BARNET DIVISION

ST JOHN AMBULANCE

THE SINKING OF HM LANDING SHIP TANK 420

AND

BARNET ST JOHN AMBULANCE MEMBERS KILLED DURING WWII

Dedicated to
St John Ambulance Member - Flying Officer Edward Herbert Francis
and all the Members of a Base Signal Radar Unit and others who were killed in what has
been described as the worst Landing Craft incident of WWII

&

The Authors Mother

Leading Aircraftswomen (Cook)

Lillian Porter (nee Kerry) 1922-1957

Who served at RAF Chigwell

INTRODUCTION

This short paper is part of my continued effort to share the rich heritage of St John Ambulance in London. This happened purely by chance when the Heritage Lead for North London Mr Stephen Kruse passed me details of Barnet Division who gave their lives during WWII. On investigating I found some interesting stories, and one that of stood out, is of Flying Officer Edward Herbert Francis based at RAF Chigwell in Essex. He was killed in what has been described as the worst Landing Craft incident of WWII, near Ostend.

The story also had a tenuous connection with my family as my late mother, Leading Aircraftswomen Lillian Porter (nee Kerry) was one of the station cooks at RAF Chigwell.

I give some basic details other members, of or associated with Barnet Division and we remember the following.

- Arthur Browne who died when the ship HMS President III (MV Empire Gem) was sunk by U-boat U66. 15 miles off the Diamond Shoals buoy, off Cape Hatteras, North Carolina.
- Victor Coleman a Sick Berth Attendant serving on HMS Aldenham (L22) a British Royal Navy Hunter Class Destroyer Type 111. She was mined and sunk in the north-eastern Adriatic Sea about 30 miles north west of Zera.
- Helen Maud Thompson, a civilian and wife of Barnet St John Ambulance member Harold George Thompson. Died 20 January 1945 aged 42 years. This was probably the (V2) Big Ben Incident 566 at Potters Bar.

ACKNOWLEDGMENTS

My thanks to Malcolm Knight OStJ of St John Ambulance (NSW), Australia who has kindly helped me with proof reading, peer review and comment on the text and Arwyn Evans. I also thank Kathryn Krause, MStJ, who reviewed the very early draft. Finally, I wish to thank Area President Squadron Leader Alan R D Clark MBE(Mil) MStJ. RAFVR(T) (Ret'd) for his support and agreeing to write the Foreword to this publication. It is only right that a Royal Air Force Officer should add a reflection to my research.

COPYRIGHT

I, Brian L Porter confirm that the work presented in this document is my own. Where information has been derived from other sources, I confirm that this has been indicated in this research paper. The right of Brian L Porter to be identified as the author of this work except where specified and acknowledged has been asserted by in accordance with the Copyright and Patents Act 1988.

Where possible I have acknowledged the source of the material used. Some, where still under copyright, it may no longer be feasible to trace the original copyright holder. I acknowledge and am grateful for use of images and material to enhance this work. Some are available for use under Creative Commons Licence, and this is stated where applicable. However, I apologise for any copyright infringement which I am happy to correct in future editions of this research paper, if advised. I am confident that, in line with advice from the British Library all the material quoted may be used for research and educational purposes.

Cover and Book design by Brian Leonard Porter No part of this book can be reproduced in any form or by written, electronic or mechanical means, including photocopying, recording, or by any information retrieval system, without written permission, in writing by the author. Published by Brian Leonard Porter

Although every precaution has been taken in the preparation of this book, the publisher and author assume no responsibility for errors or omissions. Neither is any liability assumed for damages resulting from the use of information contained herein.

Copyright © 2024 Brian Leonard Porter

All rights reserved.

ISBN   978-1-9196468-3-1

Printed by Book Printing UK www.bookprintinguk.com Remus House, Coltsfoot Drive, Peterborough, PE2 9BF

Printed in Great Britain

CONTENT

Introduction		Page 4
Acknowledgement		Page 4
Copyright		Page 5
Content		Page 6
Foreword		Page 8
Chapter One	Flying Officer Edward Herbert Francis RAFVR	Page 10
Chapter Two	RAF Chigwell	Page 17
Chapter Three	Other Barnet Members Killed in Action 1939 -1945	Page 24
Appendix One	Commonwealth War Grave Commission Edward Francis	Page 28
Appendix Two	Standardisation of Mobile Signals Units	Page 33
Appendix Three	Roll of Honour LST 420	Page 36
Prayer	Prayer for the Fallen	Page 49
Bibliography		Pag 50

FOREWORD

BY SQUADRON LEADER (RETIRED) ALAN R D CLARK MBE (MIL) MStJ MCGI MASI RAFVR(T)

November 2023

NOT ALL AIRMEN AND WOMEN FLY!

The title of the forward is an adaptation of the title of a book by Jenny Filby and Geoff Clark, no relative, called "Not All Airmen Fly – The Story of RAF Chigwell first published in 1994. Most members of the public when I am seen in uniform ask, "What do, or did you fly?" This is understandable as the "Flyers" are those readily seen either in the media or documentaries or displays by the Red Arrows. The exception being No 63 Squadron Royal Air Force Regiment "Kings Colour Squadron" and RAF Bands seen at events such as the Royal British Legion Festival of Remembrance. All these service staff have a dual role. The RAF Regiment are "first in" to secure an airfield and then maintain the security until "last out". The musicians have a medical role to play in theatres of action.

What is not seen, and this paper highlights, is the organisation behind the spectacle and day to day operational activity. The technicians that keep the aircraft in readiness, the communications teams including radar units who vector/guide aircraft to where they are needed, the administration, training, medical and catering staff.

I am grateful to Mr Brian Porter OStJ for this opportunity to acknowledge the role and sacrifice of St John members in the Royal Air Force in time of conflict and the existence of RAF Chigwell, close to where I live and walk in the now country park where some remnants of the former base are evident from "Balloon Pans", concrete roadways, anti-tank blocks and a ROC (Royal Observer Corps) bunker which is fenced off for safety reasons and the "INTONE" stone marking one operation supported by a communication and radar unit from RAF Chigwell.

This research in this paper highlights what was and remains the single largest loss of RAF personal in a single incident of service personal of all ranks from the RAF and the involvement of a St John Ambulance member.

RAF Chigwell, originally opened for manufacturing and personnel training station for "Barrage Balloon" defences for London and other cities staffed by the WAAF (Women's Auxiliary Air Force) later the WRAF (Women's Royal Air Force). As the need for balloon defences reduced, Chigwell became the main operational and training base for Communications and Radar operations. This included deployment of front-line units to ensure that as the war battles moved towards Germany the communications and Radar, which was still in its infancy, remained clear and up to date.

One such deployment saw Flying Officer (Fg Off) Edward Herbert Francis RAF VR and 202 Officers and other ranks travel across towards Dunkirk in a tank landing craft to set up such a forward operational centre. As this paper details Fg. Off. Francis and the 202 died as a result of their transport making contact with a German Sea Mine.

As many who either volunteered or were drafted, Fg Off Francis was a member of the Volunteer Reserve. During the war The RAF had four arms, The RAF, The Royal Auxiliary Air Force (AUX pins on Lapels). The Volunteer Reserve (VR pins on Lapels) the usual way into the RAF for conscripts, and from 1941 the Volunteer Reserve, Training Branch (VRT on Lapels). The Auxiliary Air Force was and is the equivalent of the Royal Naval Reserve and Territorial Army.

As both former member of the RAFVRT and now Area President for St John Ambulance I have an affinity with both organisations and those who gave their lives in conflicts past and present.

The Motto of St John Ambulance is "Pro Fide Pro Utilitate Hominum" which translates to "For the Faith and in the Service of Humanity" relieving suffering whatever the cause without fear or favour. Those who went to war, whether voluntarily or through conscription did so to protect those who cannot protect themselves from suffering under oppression, their first aid skills and knowledge would have been of great use and comfort to their comrades, civilians, and other combatants in need.

The Motto of the Royal Air Force is "Per Ardua Ad Astra", "Through Adversity to The Stars" Fg Off Francis and the 202 RAF personnel, along with other St John members who died that day elsewhere, along with others killed in action before and after, went through adversity to the peace beyond the stars.

As the Kohima Epitaph says,

"When you go home tell them of us and say, for your tomorrow we gave our today".
This and other of Brian Porters papers ensures that former members of St John Ambulance will be remembered and talked about.

WE WILL REMEMBER THEM.

Squadron Leader (Ret'd) Alan R D Clark MBE (Mil) MStJ MCGI MASI RAFVR(T)
Area President
London Borough of Redbridge and Waltham Forest.
East London District
St John Ambulance

St John Ambulance Barnet

CHAPTER ONE - FLYING OFFICER EDWARD HERBERT FRANCIS RAFVR

Edward Francis was a Private in the Barnet Division St John Ambulance prior to joining the Royal Air Force Volunteer Reserve. On examining the division's records for those killed in action we found the above-named member who had died in November 1944.

The 1911 Census shows Edward Herbert Francis was living at 8 Orchard Road Barnet, Chipping Barnet, Hertfordshire, England. His age was 6 having been born in 1905 His father was Herbert Charles Francis whose occupation was shown as an Heraldic Artist, Coachbuilders, own account. His mother was Mary Ethel Francis. He had one brother born in early 1911 named Geoffrey Charles Francis.

Edward was baptised on 28 January 1906 at Christ Church, Barnet, England.

On 14 April 1935 Edward H Francis married Esther Elisabeth Jorgensen. Esther was born in Frederiksberg, Denmark on 17 May 1907.

At the time the 1939 Register was being completed, Edward, along with his father Herbert and brother Geoffrey, were all shown as Heraldic Artists. Their mother Mary was also listed along with Esther Francis (Hart) [1,] as living at the same address – 8 Orchard Road, Barnet.

Geoffrey was noted as being a member of the Auxiliary Fire Service BUDC [Barnet Urban District Council] Driver 152, whilst Esther, Edward's wife was listed as a British Red Cross Nurse 931 BUDC [Barnet Urban District Council]

Edward, whom we are following, was recorded on the register as St John Ambulance Brigade/ 839 Stretcher Party BUDC [Barnet Urban District Council]

Edward subsequently joined the Royal Air Force Volunteer Reserve as a Flying Officer.

Having examined the records, an entry was found for Edward Herbert Francis with correct date of death 07 November 1944. Edward was then aged 38 years old and a Royal Air Force Volunteer Reserve Officer with the B.S.R.U. [Base Signal Radar Unit].

---

1 After Edwards death Esther E Francis remarried in April Qtr. 1966 someone by name of Wilfred D Hart. Esther lived Worthing and died there in the April quarter 1976. The date of birth also was a match. Source: Civil Registration Death Index

The men had been trained at Chigwell which was the RAF school for training in RADAR[2], which had already provided Mobile Signals, Radar, and Signals Servicing Units manned by British Royal Air Force personnel (2nd Tactical Air Force) who landed from Landing Craft on Omaha Beach on D-Day and successive days, and sustained significant casualties, both dead and wounded. The RAF's No.21 Base Defence Sector included the Ground Control Interception (GCI) mobile Radar Unit. Their duties were to locate enemy aircraft and to direct Fighter patrols of the RAF's 2nd Tactical Air Force to intercept them and thus provided air cover for the beaches. These units were dispersed throughout the American Sector until September 1944.

Following the D-Day landings, in November 1944, his unit was on the move toward the Essex Coast and onwards to Ostend. But unfortunately, Edwards Francis was lost as a result of an incident in which LST-420 hit a mine, exploded and broke in two at sea near the coast of Ostend, Belgium, sinking with great loss of life, particularly amongst her Royal Air Force Passengers.

LST-420 was a United States Navy LST-1- class tank landing ship that was transferred to the Royal Navy by the USA during World War Two.

LST-420 HMS (Stern) c1944
Photographer and Copyright unknown
Photograph accessed via Internet 8 August 2023 https://wrecksite.eu

---

[2] Information accessed on website 11/08/2023 www.therafatomahabeach.com

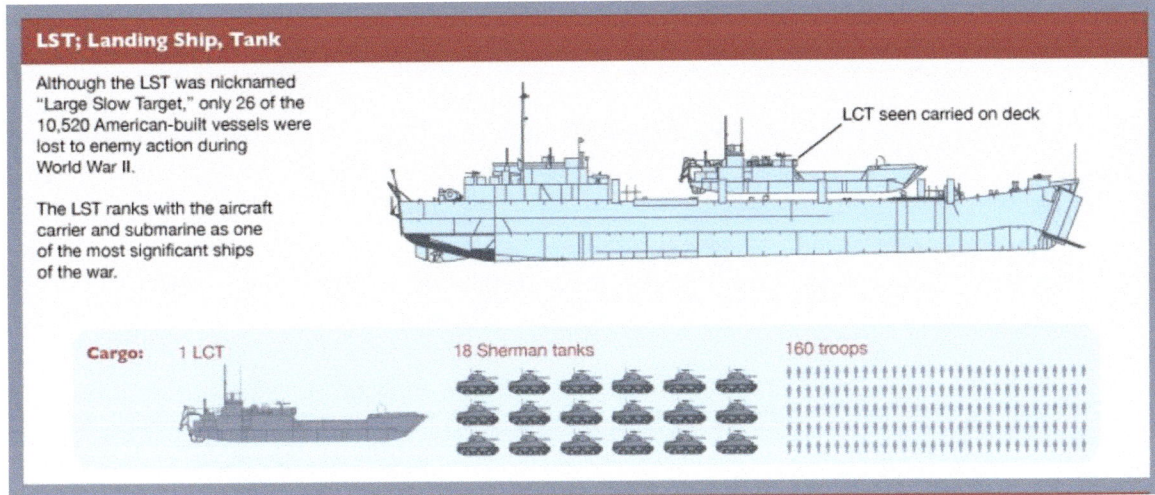

Photograph accessed via Internet 8 August 2023 courtesy of
https://www.britannica.com/technology/landing-ship-tank

The above reports shows tanks and personnel. In the incident described it was carrying Radar Units, RAF personnel and its crew. When LST-420 hit a mine off the Ostend coast in 1944. It was the greatest loss of life on a British Landing Craft during World War II. Details from website Belgians-remember-them.eu

S - Boats laying moored mines 1943

The Official War Dairy (originally marked Most Secret but now declassified) edited reports on pages 187 and 188 as follows [3] -

---

3 Internet Access http://ww2talk.com/index.php?threads/lst-420.11941/page-

Post by Michel Sabarly 20/12/2013.

MOST SECRET

187

War Diary
8.11.1944
Wednesday

HOME COMMANDS

Port Facilities

Ostend. (Contd.)   feet. Tanker with 5500 tons M.T.80. One hospital carrier. One personnel ship. 5 L.S.T. agreed P.E.C.
(N.O.I.C. Ostend, 081056 to A.N.C.X.F., Exfor, C. in C. Nore.)

Approach Channel reasonably clear of mines. Port now open and can accept ships mentioned in my 081056 tomorrow Thursday 9th a.m. tide.
(N.O.I.C. Ostend, 081816 to C. in C. Nore, A.N.C.X.F., Com. Belgium.)

L.S.T.420   L.S.Ts. 405, 367, 320 and GREENFLY with survivors ex L.S.T.420 returned and proceeded Tilbury.
(Com. Southend, 081021A to N.O.I.C. Ostend.)
Following report on loss of L.S.T.420.
(1) Ostend port closed owing to N.W. gale a.m. 7th Nov.
(2) L.S.T.420 mined in approach channel in position OD 4, 104° – 7 cables at 1539/7th.

/(3)...

188

War Diary
8.11.1944
Wednesday

HOME COMMANDS

Casualties and Defects

L.S.T.420 (Contd.)
(3) Trawlers GREENFLY despatched from anchorage to investigate at 1545.
(4) L.S.T.405 reported L.S.T.420 in 2 halves at 1649 L.S.T.320 and 367 also remained in the vicinity to pick up survivors.
(5) Accurate number of survivors not known as L.S.T. and GREENFLY returned to U.K.
(6) Stern of wreck sighted at first light a.m. Wednesday 8th and A.R.B. despatched. 1 survivor was recovered from propeller guard of wreck.
(7) Wide area searched by 2 Walrus Aircraft, 6 A.R.B. and 2 M.Ls. 36 bodies recovered names to be forwarded later.
(N.O.I.C. Ostend 082008A to A.N.C.X.F., C. in C. Nore, Admty.)

Three LSTs (LST 405, 320 & 367) and HMT Greenfly were in the area to report and pick-up survivors. HMT Greenfly, originally registered as Quantock, was a Type ASW Trawler Built. 1936 Pennant. FY156. She was built by Cochrane & Sons and Commissioned in 1939, then sold to the Admiralty on 15 November 1939. Her displacement was 441 tons and she had a speed of Speed 12 knots. At the end of the war the Admiralty sold her off.

HMT Greenfly[4]

There was also a wide area search by two Walrus Aircraft 6 Air Rescue Boats (ARB) and 2 Motor Launches (ML)

A 1943 photograph of a Walrus [5]

The following contemporary account was taken from "Aerial" Volume 2 No 4 published in September 1945

---

[4] Internet accessed 21/08/2023 – HMT Greenfly. https://www.harwichanddovercourt.co.uk/warships/trawlers/

[5] Internet accessed on 21 August 2023 https://en.wikipedia.org/wiki/Supermarine_Walrus. The Supermarine Walrus was a British single-engine amphibious biplane designed by R. J. Mitchell at their works at Woolston, Southampton.

EXTRACT TAKEN FROM "AERIAL" VOL.2 NO.4 - SEPT. 1945

In our December issue we published a short and very guarded account of a memorial service held at Chigwell. It is now possible to say that this service was in commemoration of the victims of what was possibly the worst disaster suffered by R.A.F.Signals in the whole of the Europian war.

Although others were included too, in particular the gallant members of the mobile radar unit that went down fighting to the last at Arnhem, the service was particularly dedicated to the ill fated B.S.R.U. whose home was for nearly 18 months at the Signals Battle training school. During those 18 months it not only completed its own training but also took a large part in the training and equipping of the many mobile signals and radar units which joined 2nd TAF. It was not until the second battle of France had been fought and won that it was called forward for service on the Continent and it eventually sailed for the port of Ostend on the morning of Nov.7th, 1944. The advance and near parties had already crossed in safety and were awaiting its arrival in Belgium.

During the early part of November the weather was attrocious and the unit had waited several days in the Essex marshalling area. When it did eventually sail in one LST, conditions began to deteriorate steadily and by the time the vessel was off Ostend a storm had arisen and there was a heavy sea running. In these circumstances the Captain of the LST decided, very unfortunately, as things turned out that it was unsafe to attempt a landing at Ostend, and gave orders to turn round and make for England again. It was on the return voyage, at about 3 o/c in the afternoon and while still in sight of the Belgium coast, that the vessel struck a mine amidships, was blown in two, and sank in a very short space of time. In addition to the damaging effect of the mine, the galley fires which were in use for the preparation of an evening's meal for the ship's compliment, set fire to the petrol running out of the damaged vehicles tanks, and the whole of the stern portion was rapidly enveloped in flames. The heavy seas which were running at the time prevented all but the larger vessels in the vicinity from going to the rescue, and of the 263 Officers and men on board only 32 were saved. A lesser but none the less serious loss, was that of 30% of the unit's transport which went down with the ship.

Out of the wreckage and confusion of this disaster, plain indications of individual heroism and self sacrifice plainly emerge, although it is obvious that only a fraction of the tale can ever be told. Several of those who had found a measure of safety on the rafts abandoned it to swim out to their comrades in difficulty, and were unable to get back through the heavy seas. The unit accountant Officer, F/Lt.Cleary was found tied to another Officer when recovered. The Commanding Officer who lost his life, was recovered with a bandaged head, though he had no bandage when last seen before the explosion. The beaches upon which many of the bodies were washed up were still mined at the time, and the task of retrieving them was full of danger.

There was at least one example of miraculous escape. An Airman who was asleep in his bunk immediately above the explosion of the mine, was blown straight out of the ship into the water. He lived to tell the tale.

X (Malcolm Butler, now living in Canada)

2.

Those who did not live, 13 Officers and 218 other ranks, were a grievous loss. There could have been few at Chigwell who had not lost at least one friend among them and the news of the disaster was a severe shock to the Group as a whole. The new B.S.R.U. could be and was build up on the nucleous of the old, but these men could never be replaced. The Unit was reformed at Ghent under the command of W/Co. Emery (subsequentley W/Co Melvin) All replacement personnel, survivors and essential items of equipment being flown across by Dakota Aircraft.

It carried out invaluable work in the closing stages of the European campaign, overhauling and repairing radio and radar vehicles of the 2nd. TAF, but the loss that it suffered and the men who went down on that grey November afternoon will not soon be forgotten.

Extract from *Aerial Vol 2 No 4 Sept 1945* - Contributed by Roger Smoothy for his father C/MX 107794 Leading Writer Peter Smoothy RN 9th LST Flotilla. Internet accessed 18/08/2023 http://www.navsource.org/archives/10/16/160420.htm

In the book entitled Not All Airmen Fly -The Story of RAF Chigwell by Jenny Filby and Geoff Clark[6], a brief mention is made about the incident.

> High Sprits turned to sadness in November when on the 23rd, a memorial service was held on the station for all the MSU personnel who had fallen in action and especially for the 12 officers and 220 airmen who lost their lives when their transport ship was sunk in the Channel.

The probate entry for Edward Herbert Francis is recorded in the 1945 register, as follows –

> **FRANCIS** Edward Herbert of Orchardcote 8 Orchard-road Barnet **Herfordshire** died 7 November 1944 on war service Administration **Llandudno** 31 May to Esther Elisabeth Francis widow. Effects £1150 8s. 9d.

---

[6] Not All Airmen Fly -The Story of RAF Chigwell by Jenny Filby and Geoff Clark Published by Epping Forest District Council 1994 Printed by GB Print and Graphics.

CHAPTER TWO - RAF CHIGWELL

There are few accounts of this incident I have referenced four reports which give an insight into this disaster and the losses that ensued.

The following information came to light regarding RAF Chigwell
In the *Royal Air Force Historical Society Journal,* No18, published in 1998[7] the Rt. Hon. Lord Merlyn-Rees PC[8], who had attended a training courses at Chigwell offered "Some Reflections" on his time there -

> I served from 1941 to 1946; I was 1576563 AC2 and 119433; that last number serves me in great stead and I can use that number for all sorts of things because I still remember it almost every hour of the day. I was in the University Air Squadron and that did me the world of good, that is why when I was a Minister I did my best to conserve the University Air Squadrons.
>
> We had had a training course at RAF Chigwell, which was a balloon station, and the conditions at Chigwell were really quite extraordinary – thousands of us living in a balloon hanger with beds which seemed to go up and up. What I did not know at the time was that complaints were made in Parliament, but I did not read the newspapers in those days and certainly did not listen to the radio. I went and had a look at Hansard the other day, for early 1942, but could not find any record of it, although I am told there were great complaints about it and the conditions were not of the best. I suppose they were saying well they will not be of the best where you are going, if they had told us where we were going.

RAF Chigwell was opened in May 1938[9] as No.4 Balloon Centre covering north east London. Occupying nearly 70 acres the Station was well equipped. Five Balloon storage sheds, three large vehicle hangers, twenty billet huts for personnel, NAAFI, Post Office, Chapel and Sick Bay and over 100 smaller buildings

Three Royal Auxiliary Air Force Balloon Squadrons were based there - 908 (County of Essex), 909 (County of Essex) and 910 (County of Essex), and were part of 30 Group. They were responsible for manufacturing the balloons out of 24 separate panels and six rigging wires as well as testing and maintaining them until 1943. The total London barrage consisted of 450 balloons.

On 1st April 1943 No 4 Balloon Centre was re-designated RAF Chigwell under the control of 26 group. As, from 1943-45, RAF Chigwell had been the country's main base for the formation, equipping and final training of Mobile Signal Units.[10] The camp was home to some 3600 people. In September of that year, a number of mobile Ground Control Interception (GCI) radar teams began to be trained in preparation for the Normandy landings and the campaign across Europe as part of the 2nd Tactical Air Force.

---

7 Royal Air Force Historical Society Journal 18 ISBN 13614231 1998 Printed by Fotodirect Ltd.

8 Merlyn Merlyn-Rees, Baron Merlyn-Rees, PC (né Merlyn Rees; 18 December 1920 – 5 January 2006) was a British Labour Party politician and Member of Parliament from 1963 until 1992. He served as Secretart of State for Northern Ireland (1974–1976) and Home Secretary (1976–1979). He was also for a time Parliamentary Under-Secretary (Ministry of Defence) (Air Force) Ministry of Defence 16 April 1966 - 1 November 1968

9 The Spirit of North Weald -Tying up lose ends about Units Places and Aircraft Booklet No 8 Epping Forest District Council

10 Ibid Not All Airmen Fly -The Story of RAF Chigwell

On D-Day 15082 GCI of 21 Base Defence Sector along with its Mobile Signals Unit and an additional Light Warning Set radar, was attached to the US forces and landed on Omaha Beach, suffering 48 dead and wounded out of 180 airmen, NCOs and officers, with only 8 out of 27 vehicles getting off the beach. Their blue battledress uniforms attracted fire from both the Germans and Americans. The unit claimed its first kill on 10 June, along with a probability.

Air Commodore Leslie Dalton Morris later Air Marshal Sir Leslie Dalton-Morris KBE, CB MID Photograph by Walter Bird, bromide print, 9 November 1961 CCL NPG x166974 © National Portrait Gallery, London

Leslie Dalton Morris was early Identified with research into Radio Detection Finding, the forerunner of radar upon which the defence of the country was founded.

On 17 August 1943 Leslie Dalton Morris[11] was promoted to Acting Air Commodore and took up new duties as the Senior Air Staff Officer at No 26 (Signals) Group, which controlled British Radar stations. He went from there to form the first mobile base signals and radar units. He also formed and commanded the Signals Battle Training School at RAF Chigwell, from which were turned out all the mobile signal units used in the invasions North Africa and Normandy[12] For this work he was awarded a CBE on 8 June 1944. He was promoted to Air Commodore on 1 October 1944, and became the youngest technical officer of Air Rank[13].

In 1958 the Air Ministry issued a restricted document Air Publication 3237, which had since been declassified. It covered signals during WWII. Volume I covered Organisation and Development, whilst Volume II dealt with Telecommunications.

The report covers further expansion at RAF Chigwell. It states on page 29 -

---

11 Air Marshal Sir Leslie Dalton Morris, KBE, CB (7 April 1906 – 28 October 1976) was a senior Royal Air Force (RAF) commander in the middle of the twentieth century. He played a leading role in the use of signals in the Air Force both during and after WWII.

12 30 December 1949 Ballymena Weekly Telegraph Ballymena, Antrim, Northern Ireland

13 11 April 1947 Hampshire Telegraph Portsmouth, Hampshire, England

Between August 1942 and June 1943, the activities of No: 26 Group expanded rapidly[14]. In 1943 No. 26 Group took on additional functions. It was responsible for the formation, equipping, operating, training and preparation for overseas operations of all mobile signal units. This involved taking over Royal Air Force Chigwell on 1 April 1943, where there were Personnel Despatch Centre (P.D.C.) facilities for 4,000. It undertook the equipping, of all field training and preparation for overseas of all m-0bile radar units. All arrangements for the preparation and training of the signals personnel of overseas forces including P.D.C. action were in the care of the group. In connection with these commitments 250 officers and 8,300 other ranks passed through Chigwell between September 1942 and June 1943 and were formed into units and despatched overseas by the group. There was a heavy increase in the responsibilities of No. 26 Group in other directions. In l943 it became responsible for the Signals Development Unit, Hinton in- the-Hedges, consisting of the Beam Approach Development Unit, No. 1551 Beam Approach Calibration Flight, the Operational Development Flight, and No. 1478 Flight consisting of five flying W / T stations. The group als0 undertook the administrative and technical aircraft responsibility for No. 105 (Combined Operations} Wing and its training stations, and No. 516 Squadron. Also, in 1943 the group took on the responsibility for the servicing and repair of all M.F. beacons and radio track guides. In late 1942 No. 26 Group had to undertake a considerable amount of development work, to do which an additional department was formed at headquarters No. 26 Group consisting of civilian technical personnel drawn from the R.A.E., the Air Ministry and civilian sources. In June 1943 No. 26 Group was accorded command status in respect of servicing of aircraft within the group, allotment of aircraft belonging to the group and aircraft establishment of the group. This was done because the administration, servicing and flying discipline of certain units in No. 26 Group was considered unsatisfactory. The proposal that it should have command status for flying discipline was agreed to only in part.

The report continued on page 31 –

Battle Training School

One lesson learnt from the 1939-1940 campaign in France was the need for mobile and self-contained signals and radar units as an integral part of an expeditionary force. A t the beginning of the war selection and training of personnel in the use of specialist vehicles and instruction in the use of appropriate weapons of assault and defence were undertaken at White Waltham. By April 1943 commitments had grown to such an extent that the entire unit moved to Chigwell, using White Waltham as a satellite. The P.D.C. was formed in May 1943 within the framework of the Battle Training School to supervise the preparation and formation of the various units under training. From April 1943 to D-Day the main output from Chigwell was to A.E.A.F. formations, the peak effort being in the second quarter of 1944 immediately before the landings in Normandy. In addition, Chigwell under- took the formation and training of hundreds of other units for special operations all over the world. Over 70000 personnel passed through White Waltham and Chigwell and of these 52000 were trained and kitted for such theatres of war as India, Iceland, Norway, North Africa, Sicily, Italy, Russia, Yalta, Azores, Middle East, Western Europe and many countries in the Far East. After l April l943, 900 Units were fully equipped and over 3,200 specialist signals vehicles, 1,180 specialist radar vehicles and 2,600 load vehicles were sent out.

The final reference to the Base Signals Unit is to be found on page 131

Base Signals Unit Chigwell. (25 officers, 290 other ranks)
Base organisation for the installation and servicing of ground signals and R.D.F. equipment. It was intended, however, that This unit should not perform its role until in the field. In the

---

[14] See Refers to Appendix No. 4 of same report for comparison of No. 26 Group in February 1942 and June 1943.

U.K. the unit was based at R.A.F. Chigwell, which unit it was assisting to train signals personnel.

WW2 Talk Com [15] Website details Radar Services during the Winter 1944-1945.

During November 1944, under severe winter conditions, there was a relative stability of the war situation in north-west Europe. This did not mean any respite in the raid reporting work of the radar units, deployed in the main in exposed and remote localities in Holland arid Belgium. Opportunity was taken of the comparative lull in air operations to overhaul the radar equipment and carry out minor modifications which were detailed by Command Headquarters. This was achieved by taking one complete set of Ground Control Intercepts (G.C.I) equipment off the air at a time, the unit continuing to operate on the remaining types at their disposal. The Mobile Signals Servicing Units (M.S.S.U.) carried out these servicing tasks, which were beyond the capacity of unit mechanics, during their quarterly overhauls. The M.S.S.U.s were able to cope successfully with the work, even changing unserviceable turntables of the rotating aerial systems of some two tons in weight, by hand.

It had originally been planned before Operation "Neptune" (D. Day) that the Base Signals and Radar Unit B.S.R.U.) would be phased in as soon as the Normandy bridgehead had expanded sufficiently for the base area to be regarded as safe for such large units. However, the speed of the advance across France had been so great and the M.S.S.U.s were functioning so well that the B.S.R.U. was held in the United Kingdom until a suitable site could be selected in Belgium. Meetings were held both at Air Ministry and at Headquarters, Second Tactical Air Force, during October 1944, when consideration was given to the question of whether the B.S.R.U. was really necessary. A decision was taken that the unit was required in the base area on the Continent but its establishment was revised and decreased from 450 to 303 personnel. After considerable delays, occasioned in the first place by weather and later by the Walcheren Island operations to clear the approaches to Antwerp, the main body of No. 1 B.S.R.U. and the greater part of its vehicles and equipment were embarked in a Landing Ship, Tank (L.S.T.) for Ostend. Heavy seas were running on 7 November when the unit sailed and, within sight of Ostend, the vessel struck a mine at 1500 hours and sank quickly. Of the B.S.R.U. complement on board, 14 officers, 224 other ranks and 50 vehicles loaded with equipment were lost -- only five officers and 26 other ranks were saved.

This heavy loss was rendered more tragic when considered in relation to the very large number of signals personnel and the enormous quantities of radar and signals equipment which had been transported to the Continent during the five months since D-day without loss. When it is recalled that the total revised establishment of the unit was 303 personnel the magnitude of the loss can be appreciated. In effect it meant that the unit had to be reformed completely in the shortest possible time. It was agreed that the unit should be reformed on the Continent and not in the United Kingdom. The work was started immediately, the personnel rendered surplus by the earlier reduction in the B.S.R.U. establishment were recalled, so that the unit began again with a good nucleus of experienced personnel.

---

15 WW2 Talk.Com Website accessed on 19 August 2023 Entry by username Andy P538
http://ww2talk.com/index.php?threads/lst-420.11941/page-3

Official Badge of Second Tactical Air Force

Background for final operations[16]. The weather was very poor and had resulted in a relative lull in aerial fighting in North West Europe. This presented the 2nd Tactical Air Force with an opportunity to conduct necessary servicing, repairs and overhaul of radar installations in North West Europe as "partial downtime" was unavoidable in the process and the defence could not be "down" when the Luftwaffe was active. The process involved taking a radar installation "off line" but leaving the site still functioning on its alternative systems.

All such major maintenance after the D-Day landings on 6 June 1944, until November 1944, had been accomplished by small "Mobile Signals Servicing Units" (MSSU) which had been enormously successful. The tactical plan was for the "No. 1 Base Signals and Radar Unit" (BSRU), which had completed eighteen months training at the Signals Base Training School [RAF Chigwell], to land in France once the Normandy bridgehead was sufficiently stable but due to the MSSU's success and the greater rate of territorial advance than expected, the BSRU had been held in England until a more suitable time.

After meetings at the Air Ministry in London and the 2nd Tactical Air Force HQ in North West Europe, it was decided to move the unit, its vehicles and personnel to a site at Ghent, Belgium where workshops were set up and equipment began to arrive. On receipt of movement orders in the marshalling area in Essex, the 303 men of the unit began boarding *LST-420* which took aboard 19 officers and 250 personnel of No. 1 BSRU (some sources say 263 officers and men) with their 50 vehicles, equipment and supplies, the remaining officer and 33 men boarded another LST with several of their vehicles.

Loss. On 7 November 1944, a small convoy of vessels comprising LST-200, LST320, LST-367, LST-405 and *LST-420* crossed the English Channel bound for Ostend, Belgium. The weather had been very poor for a week and a severe storm was rising. By mid-afternoon when they arrived off the Belgian coast conditions were terrible, and as a result they were refused permission to enter port at Ostend due to concerns that an accident in the harbourmouth might cause considerable disruption in the supply line for land forces. The convoy duly altered course back towards England planning to shelter overnight in the Thames Estuary before returning to Ostend on the following day.

---

16 Internet Wikipedia was accessed on the 8 August 2023

A Landing Ship Tank at the Wharf, St Peter Port, Guernsey - May 1945
A landing ship with her bow doors open looms over a large crowd assembled on the quay[17].

The only surviving Landing Craft Tank LCT 7074, is on display at Southsea Seafront it is the last surviving vessel of its type.

At approximately 15:00, within sight of Ostend the bow section of *LST-420* struck a German mine which tore a large hole in the ship's hull causing it to break into two parts. The ship's galley fires were lit at the time due to the evening meal being prepared and gallons of petrol from the damaged fuel tanks of the vehicles caught fire enveloping the stern section of the ship in flame. *LST-420* sank very rapidly and due to the heavy seas only larger vessels were able to attempt to rescue survivors in the water. Only 31 or 32 men of the BSRU were saved from life rafts.

The position of the wreck is recorded as 51°15.033'N 2° 41.798'E.[8] A section of the bow of *LST-420* was raised in 1990. A yellow marker buoy is located above the wreck today.

Casualties. Crew – Lieutenant-Commander Douglas Everett, and 54 other members of the crew of *LST-40* were lost that night. (4 are buried in Belgium, 1 was washed ashore in England and was taken home for burial by his family. The other members of the crew are commemorated on the Naval Memorials at Plymouth, Chatham and the Royal New Zealand Naval Memorial).

---

17 IWM ART LD 559 by Harold William Hailstone

Runnymede Memorial where at least 136 of the casualties of *LST-420* are commemorate

The dead are buried mainly at Ostend and Blankenberge but as far north as Kiel in Germany. Those without graves are commemorated on the Runnymede Memorial. The majority were members of "No.1 BSRU".

- Other passengers – it is possible that 12 members of No. 335 Provost Company, "Corps of Military Police" Royal Military Police, 6 members of No. 111 General Hospital, Royal Army Medical Corps, 9 members of Royal Army Service Corps and several other British Army personnel were also lost aboard *LST-420*.

	Total Recorded	RAF, RCAF & AAF	RAF & RCAF OFFICERS	WO RAF	RAF Flg Sgt & Sgt	RAF Jr/Ranks	LC- Captain, Officers & Crew	335 Provost CO RMP	No 111 General Hospital RAMC	Royal Army Service Corps	Others (2RE & 1 ACC)
Total Listed Below Varified by CWGC Records	320		14	3	27	191	55	12	6	9	3
Killed on 7 November 1944 En.Wikipedia.org	318		14	3	31	189	55	12	5	9	0
Bulletin Air War (Dutch War Magazine) -WW2talk.com	312	226					55	12	8	8	3
Personel rescued saved -WW2talk.com	31		5			26	0				
E&OE											

Losses vary from report to report. However, the total loss of life recorded by the Commonwealth War Graves Commission is 320. The dead were washed ashore as far north as the north German coast, on the beaches of the Netherlands, Belgium, England and as far south as Calais, France.

CHAPTER THREE - BARNET DIVISION MEMBERS KILLED IN ACTION

In Memory of Able Seaman

ARTHUR HARRY BROWNE

Service Number: P/JX 289207

H.M.S. President III (M.V. Empire Gem), Royal Navy who died on 24 January 1942. Age 21. Son of Albert and Mary Browne, of New Barnet, Hertfordshire.

Remembered with Honour

PORTSMOUTH NAVAL MEMORIAL

Panel 63, Column 2. [18] [19]

COMMEMORATED IN PERPETUITY BY THE COMMONWEALTH WAR GRAVES COMMISSION

Arthur Browne was living with parents in New Barnet when he died on 24 January 1942. Aged 21 years. Royal Navy HMS President III[20] (MV Empire Gem), Browne was listed as an Able Seaman (Defensively Armed Merchant Ships (DAMS) gunner).[21]

At 02.40 hours on 24 Jan 1942 the unescorted **Empire Gem,** a Motor Tanker, (Master Francis Reginald Broad) was hit amidships and aft by two torpedoes from U-66 15 mile southeast of the Diamond Shoals buoy off Cape Hatteras, North Carolina. The tanker immediately caught fire and later broke in two and sank in 35°02N/75°33W. 43 crew members and six gunners were lost. The master and the radio operator were picked up by a US Coast Guard vessel and landed at Hatteras Inlet on 25 January.

Empire Gem following attack by U-boat U66
Photograph Courtesy of the National Archives - Source https://monitor.noaa.gov/shipwrecks/empire_gem.html

---

18 https://www.cwgc.org/find-records/find-war-dead/casualty-details/2368703/arthur-harry-browne/

19 https://www.cwgc.org/visit-us/find-cemeteries-memorials/cemetery-details/144703/portsmouth-naval-memorial/

20 HMS President III was a shore pay and administration office for men serving in (*inter* alia)Defensivley Armed Merchant Ships (DAMS).

21 Internet accessed 21 August 2023 Details from www.uboat.net

In Memory Of Sick Berth Attendant

VICTOR COLEMAN

Service Number: P/MX 84558

H.M.S. Aldenham., Royal Navy who died on 14 December 1944

Remembered with Honour

PORTSMOUTH NAVAL MEMORIAL

Panel 87, Column 1. [22] [23]

COMMEMORATED IN PERPETUITY BY THE COMMONWEALTH WAR GRAVES COMMISSION

Victor Coleman, a Sick Berth Attendant No P/MX 84558 was serving on HMS Aldenham with correct date. Date of Death 14 December 1944. Age not stated. HMS Aldenham (L22) was a British Royal Navy Hunter Class Destroyer Type III. She was mined and sunk in the north-eastern Adriatic Sea about 30 miles north west of Zera. Five officers and 121 ratings killed. Five officers (including the CO) and 58 ratings picked up by HMS Atherstone[24].

HMS Aldenham L22
This photograph FL 412 Is from the Imperial War Museums (Collection No 8308-29)

---

[22] https://www.cwgc.org/find-records/find-war-dead/casualty-details/2369596/victor-coleman/

[23] https://www.cwgc.org/visit-us/find-cemeteries-memorials/cemetery-details/144703/portsmouth-naval-memorial/

[24] Internet accessed on 21/08/2023 Websites www.wrecksite.eu and www.uboat.net

In Memory Of Civilian

HELEN MAUD THOMPSON

Civilian War Dead who died on 20 January 1945 Age 42
of 55 Southgate Road. Wife of Harold George Thompson. Died at 55 Southgate Road.

Remembered with Honour

POTTERS BAR, URBAN DISTRICT [25] [26]

COMMEMORATED IN PERPETUITY BY THE COMMONWEALTH WAR GRAVES COMMISSION

Helen Maud Thompson was a Civilian and wife of Barnet St John Ambulance member Harold George Thompson. Date of Death 20 January 1945. Age 42 years.

This incident probably refers to (V2) Big Ben Incident 566 at Potters Bar 10.52 hrs on Sunday 20 January 1945. This incident resulted in 21 killed and 26 badly hurt.[27]

---

25 https://www.cwgc.org/find-records/find-war-dead/casualty-details/3144503/helen-maud-thompson/

26 https://www.cwgc.org/visit-us/find-cemeteries-memorials/cemetery-details/4004896/potters-bar-urban-district/

27 *The Blitz then and Now* Volume 3 ISBN 0900913 58 4 Printers Plaistow Press Editor Winston G Ramsey.

APPENDIX ONE

COMMONWEALTH WAR GRAVE COMMISSION

AND FIND A GRAVE RECORDS FOR

EDWARD HERBERT FRANCIS[28]

In Memory Of
Flying Officer

EDWARD HERBERT FRANCIS

Service Number: 144497

B.S.R.U., Royal Air Force Volunteer Reserve who died on 07 November 1944 Age 38

Son of Herbert Charles and Mary Ethel Francis; husband of Esther Elisabeth Francis, of Worthing, Sussex

Remembered with Honour

OOSTENDE NEW COMMUNAL CEMETERY

Plot 9. Row 2. Grave 6.

COMMONWEALTH WAR GRAVES

COMMEMORATED IN PERPETUITY BY THE COMMONWEALTH
WAR GRAVES COMMISSION

---

[28] https://www.cwgc.org/find-records/find-war-dead/casualty-details/2081934/edward-herbert-francis/

FAWCETT, Marine JOSEPH, PLY/X. 109226. Royal Marines. No. 47 R.M. Commando. 7th November, 1944. Age 20. Son of Mr. and Mrs. H. Fawcett, of Liverpool. Plot 9. Row 7. Grave 13.

FIELD, Pilot Offr. (Pilot) MAX LIGHTFOOT, 119347. R.A.F. (V.R.). 149 Sqdn. 16th April, 1942. Age 20. Son of Henry and Ada Nellie Field, of Cambridge. Plot 9. Row 4. Joint grave 22-23.

FISHER, Second Offr. ROBERT ROWLANDS, Merchant Navy. S.S. *Samsip* (London). 7th December, 1944. Age 29. Son of James Faulds Fisher, and of Minnie Fisher, of Wallasey, Cheshire. Plot 9. Row 8. Grave 2.

FISK, Tpr. ALBERT ARTHUR, 14284873. 11th Royal Tank Regt., R.A.C. 1st November, 1944. Age 31. Plot 9. Row 6. Grave 34.

FITZGERALD, Pte. EDWARD, 5436014. 2nd Bn. The Duke of Cornwall's Light Infantry. 3rd June, 1940. Age 27. Son of Edward and Bridget Fitzgerald, of Ardfert, Co. Kerry, Irish Republic. Plot 9. Row 3. Grave 39.

FITZ JOHN, Gnr. JOHN WILLIAM, 14657062. 73 Lt. A.A. Regt., Royal Artillery. 20th January, 1945. Age 20. Son of James Charles and Rose Alice Fitz John, of Islington, London. Plot 9. Row 8. Grave 27.

FOSKETT, Pte. EDWARD FREDERICK, 5678714. 5/7th Bn. The Gordon Highlanders. 1st October, 1945. Age 25. Son of Frederick John Joseph and Emily Foskett, of Mottingham, London; husband of Doris Eileen Foskett, of Petts Wood, Kent. Plot 9. Row 11. Grave 41.

FRANCIS, Flying Offr. EDWARD HERBERT, 144497. R.A.F. (V.R.). 7th November, 1944. Age 38. Son of Herbert Charles and Mary Ethel Francis; husband of Esther Elisabeth Francis, of Worthing, Sussex. Plot 9. Row 2. Grave 6.

FRANCIS, Seaman GEORGE VICTOR CYRIL, LT/JX. 190173. R.N. Patrol Service. H.M. Trawler *Elizabeth Angela*. 13th August, 1940. Age 27. Husband of L. M. Francis, of Beccles, Suffolk. Plot 9. Row 3. Grave 21.

FRITH, Fus. FREDERICK DONALD, 6460582. 2nd Bn. The Royal Fusiliers (City of London Regt.). 3rd June, 1940. Age 18. Son of James and Florence Frith, of Stanwell, Middlesex. Plot 9. Row 3. Grave 41.

FYLES, Sto. 1st Cl. WILLIAM EDWARD, C/KX. 135552. R.N. H.M.L.C.T. 650. 1st November, 1944. Age 21. Son of Edward and Margaret Fyles, of Southport, Lancashire. Plot 9. Row 6. Grave 23.

GALBRAITH, Lieut. NORMAN JAMES, Twice mentioned in Despatches. R.N.V.R. ~~H.M.S. St. Christopher.~~ HM MTB 762 14th February, 1945. Age 31. Son of Colin James Galbraith and Florence Ruth Galbraith, of Exeter. Plot 9. Row 9. Grave 11.

GATES, L.A.C. JOHN THOMAS, 1783116. R.A.F. (V.R.). 7th November, 1944. Age 21. Son of William H. and Gertrude Gates, of Richmond, Yorkshire. Plot 9. Row 2. Grave 34.

GIBBS, Spr. LEONARD, 14544175. 232 Army Troops Coy., Royal Engineers. 26th November, 1944. Age 38. Husband of Hilda May Choyce Gibbs, of Nuneaton, Warwickshire. Plot 9. Row 7. Grave 38.

GIBSON, E.R.A. 4th Cl. JOHN, D/MX. 102960. R.N. H.M.L.S.T. 420. 7th November, 1944. Age 22. Son of John William and Eva Mary Gibson, of Widnes, Lancashire. Plot 9. Row 8. Grave 20.

GILLINGS, Cpl. BERT, T/1686012. R.A.S.C. 27th May, 1945. Age 27. Son of Eric Walker Gillings and Florence Betsy Gillings; husband of Florence Gillings, of Metheringham, Lincolnshire. Plot 9. Row 11. Grave 21.

GILMOUR, Pte. ROBERT, 2938534. 147 Coy., Pioneer Corps. 9th December, 1944. Age 32. Son of Archibald and Jane Wilkie Gilmour, of Peebles; husband of Mary Margaret Gilmour, of Peebles. Plot 9. Row 8. Grave 4.

GODKIN, Capt. NOEL HERBERT, M.B.E. Royal Marines. No. 48 R.M. Commando. 4th November, 1944. Age 32. Son of Herbert and Emily Mary Godkin, of Loughborough, Leicestershire. A.C.A. Plot 9. Row 7. Grave 5.

GORDON, Spr. DONALD, 1903624. Royal Engineers. 18th November, 1944. Age 26. Plot 9. Row 7. Grave 34.

OSTENDE NEW COMMUNAL CEMETERY BEL. 1.

Grave Registration Book[29]

---

[29] https://www.cwgc.org/find-records/find-war-dead/casualty-details/2081934/edward-herbert-francis/#&gid=1&pid=1

Graves Registration Report Form.

ORIGINAL

COUNTRY: BELGIUM.
COMMUNE: ~~XXXXXXX~~
REPORT No. :
SCHEDULE No. : 1.
PLACE OF BURIAL : OSTENDE NEW COMMUNAL CEMETERY, BELGIUM.
Land belongs to

Certified complete and correct.

The following are buried here :—
Signature _____ Date 30 NOV 1954

P.R.G.	No. and Rank		Initials, Name and Honours		Unit	Date of Death	For works use
IX.2.1.			UNKNOWN	AIRMAN	Royal Air Force	8.11.44.	C.H.
IX.2.2.			UNKNOWN	SAILOR	Royal Navy	13.11.44.	C.H.
IX.2.3.	53530	F/O.	L.E.	GREGORY	Royal Air Force	7.11.44.	C.H.
IX.2.4.	1195039	L.A.C.	G.F.	POOLE	Royal Air Force	7.11.44.	C.H.
IX.2.5.	Wing Commander		W.E.	WENDON	Royal Air Force	7.11.44.	C.H.
IX.2.6.	144497	F/O.	E.H.	FRANCIS	Royal Air Force	7.11.44.	C.H.
IX.2.7.	116644	Flt./Lt.	L.J.	TYLER	Royal Air Force	7.11.44.	C.H.
IX.2.8.	356672	W.O.	W.H.	REDDING	Royal Air Force	7.11.44.	C.H.
IX.2.9.	1044711	A.C.1.	G.B.	BROWN	Royal Air Force	7.11.44.	C.H.
IX.2.10.	1777211	L.A.C.	M.	BROWN	Royal Air Force	7.11.44.	C.H.
IX.2.11.	1228291	L.A.C.	A.J.	RUDDERHAM	Royal Air Force	7.11.44.	C.H.
IX.2.12.	1037904	L.A.C.	J.H.	SHICKLE	Royal Air Force	7.11.44.	C.H.
IX.2.13.	1173437	L.A.C.	W.E.	WHEELER	Royal Air Force	7.11.44.	C.H.
IX.2.14.	1488831	A.C.2.	D.I.	HUGHES	Royal Air Force	7.11.44.	C.H.
IX.2.15.	1503090	A.C.1.	R.	SHINGLER	Royal Air Force	7.11.44.	C.H.
IX.2.16.	1240020	Cpl.	R.R.	COOMBES	Royal Air Force	7.11.44.	C.H.
IX.2.17.	1410535	L.A.C.	J.C.	DAVIES	Royal Air Force	7.11.44.	C.H.
IX.2.18.	14592982	Pte.	L.W.G.	CAISLEY	Royal Army Medical Corps.	7.11.44.	C.H.

Grave Registration Report[30]

---

30 https://www.cwgc.org/find-records/find-war-dead/casualty-details/2081934/edward-herbert-francis/#&gid=1&pid=2

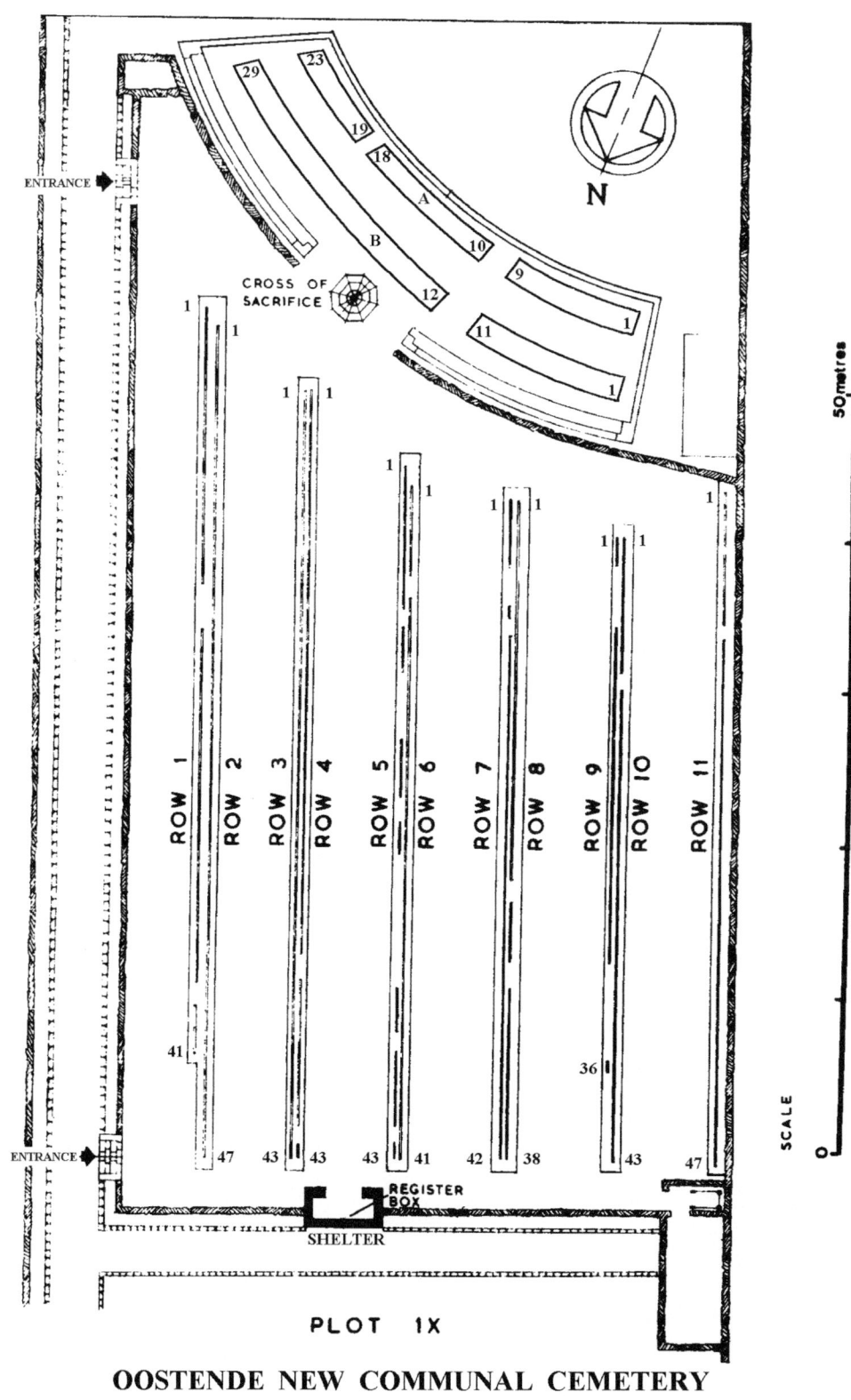

Map - OOSTENDE NEW COMMUNAL CEMETERY[31]

---

31 https://www.cwgc.org/visit-us/find-cemeteries-memorials/cemetery-details/16305/oostende-new-communal-cemetery/

Courtesy of Find a Grave[32]

Edward Herbert Francis's entry in the UK, World War II Index to Allied Airmen Roll of Honour, 1939-1945.

Name	Edward Herbert Francis	Rank	Fg Off
Death Age	38	Birth Year	abt 1906
Death Date	7 Nov 1944	Military Base	In Transit
Service Number	144497		
Unit	Base Signals & Radar Unit	Command	Lst 420
Casualty	Killed in Action Sea	Residential Place	Worthing, Sussex
Burial Place	Oostende New Communal Cemetery		
Notes	Lost in the Landing Ship Tank LST420, which was sunk when it hit a mine Near the Middelkerke Bank in bad weather off Ostend, Belgium.		

---

32 https://www.findagrave.com/memorial/13947163/edward-herbert-francis?_gl=1*i3qggt*_gcl_au*MjE3OTMwNjE1LjE2OTE1MTU5MzE.*_ga*MTY3ODQ0MTcwLjE2OTE1MTU5MzI.*_ga_4QT8FMEX30*MzkyMzc0OTAtMDFmOC00ODQyLWFiOWQtOThhMjZlOTZhNWE1LjEuMS4xNjkxNTE3MTE0LjU4LjAuMA..

APPENDIX TWO

Standardisation of Mobile Signals Units[33]

The need for standardisation of Mobile Signals Units in all theatres was evident by 1943. Only by adopting this system could the necessary training be given to persons before going overseas. Basic training was not enough; it was most important that special training should be given to airmen who were to be employed on this type of work, and such training could only be given satisfactorily if they were crewed up as complete units before despatch overseas. The difficulty was that MSUs were built up of component vehicles, the contents of which had hitherto been determined to some extent by local requirements. Some of the units in use at Home were not necessarily suitable for general adoption.

However, it was possible to agree many existing types as standard, and special vehicle types were referred to the Air Ministry who allotted the new vehicle a type number and published it to all concerned.

The Tactical Air Force which was being prepared in the United Kingdom for operations on the Continent, was the prototype for the mobile signals unit system and was planned to include advanced and rear air headquarters, base signals units, two composite groups (fighter and close support bomber), one light bomber group and one reconnaissance wing. The base signals units (BSU), mobile signals units (MSU), and mobile signals servicing units, (MSSU) together comprised a complete signals organisation for an air force in the field. Provision was made, with the addition of advanced landing ground signals sections (ALGSS) and field force headquarters signals sections (FFHQSS) for the preliminary assault stage. With slight modifications to establishment, the BSU could become the keystone of a static signals establishment.

The signals facilities for Advanced and Rear Air Headquarters and for all groups were provided by MSUs. Composite groups included a mobile operations room unit (MORU) and a mobile air reporting unit (MARU) complete with their own mobile signals sections, wireless unit screen and AME stations. Composite groups were allotted MSUs to meet the requirements of their own advanced and rear headquarters, airfields, air stores parks (ASPs) and repair and salvage units (RSUs); an MSSU; and one or more FFHQSS and ALGSS. The light bomber group was allotted MSUs in accordance with its requirements. The policy was to allot a BSU to a formation of three groups, as was the case with TAF.

The terms of reference of the BSUs were:

a) The receipt and testing of all signals and radar equipment consigned to the theatre prior to issue to units in the field.
b) The servicing of equipment returned to base as beyond the capacity of the MSSUs.
c) The holding of reserve signals and radar units.
d) The installation of fixed signals and radar stations.
e) The fitting of approved modifications.

---

[33] Copyright © 2023 The RAF at Omaha Beach.- info@therafatomahabeach.com – used with permission.

f) The development and manufacture of apparatus to meet special requirements.
g) The examination and analysis of technical reports from units and the transmission of summaries thereof to the Air Ministry.

A base signals unit was formed at Chigwell, fully mobile as part of TAF (Tactical Air Force). It was employed from June 1943 on the task of assembling and training mobile signals and radar units for despatch overseas, either immediately (as for "Husky") or as part of TAF.

The MSSUs were intended to move into an operational theatre at as early a stage as possible. They held three months' spares for MSUs and mobile radar units, and constituted the sole servicing and holding unit for such technical equipment until the BSU was established.

The work of preparing and despatching mobile units at Chigwell was carried out in three sections, the first for assembling, testing and issuing technical gear; the second for servicing, testing and issuing MT and motor cycles, and the third for issuing barrack pack-ups. Training was given in Morse and procedure, and in practical work, carried out in a hangar in which were mounted, side by side, the chassis of all types of signals vehicles. Crews were assembled, equipped and trained as a team, every effort being made to fit them for overseas conditions and for mobile operations. Instructions were given to officers on the task of administration in the field.

By the middle of 1943, a total of 16 types of mobile signals unit had been laid down by the Air Ministry, each providing standard signals facilities according to its type. The types were designed to fit together, like building blocks, into any likely total of requirements. Not all these types had been formed by June 1943, but a large number of standard types of MSU were in use by 1944, each providing different facilities. The units were numbered in four series, according to their function, as follows:

a) MSUs type "A" to "Z". These constituted the first series of MSUs to be formed. The signals equipment used was the same as that used for the transportable units, with a number of additions. The units were allocated identification letters consecutively in the order of their function, as:

Type:
"A"–8 low power HF W/T channels.
"B"–4 low power HF W/T channels (reinforcement).
"C"–4 very low power HF W/T channels.
"D"–2 low power HF W/T channels.
"E"–4 low power HF W/T channels (reinforcement).
"F"–2 very low power R/T W/T channels (reinforcement).
"G"–2 very low power HF W/T channels (reinforcement).
"H"–4 VHF R/T point-to-point channels.
"J"–VHF R/T point-to-point channel.
"K"–1 very low power HF W/T channel.
"L"–1 HF D/F channel.
"M"–1 MF beacon.
"N"–1 Radio Track Guide.
"O"–4 VHF R/T channels.

"P"–2 VHF R/T channels.
"Q"–1 VHF D/F channel.
"R"–1 high power HF W/T channel (reinforcement).
"S"–1 10 watt simplex VHF channel.
"T"–1 50 watt simplex VHF channel.
"U"–1 50 watt duplex VHF channel.
"W"–1 500 watt duplex speech plus teleprinter channel.

On the completion of this series, it was decided to sub-divide additional types of units into three double-letter series, as listed in b), c) and d) below:

b) MSUs type "CA"… "CZ". This series comprised units designed to provide communications facilities.

c) MSUs type "RA"…"RZ". This series comprised mobile radar units other than AMES.

d) MSUs type "SA"… "SZ". This series comprised units designed to provide special facilities (eg RCM) outside those covered in types "CA" to "CZ" and "RA" to "RZ".

By the end of the year, double letter types already formed included "CA" (high power speech plus teleprinter twin channel relay units); "RA" (mobile Eureka "H" beacons); "RJ" (enemy jamming investigator units); "SJ", "SM" and "SR" (RCM units); and "SS" (mobile signal security units). Other miscellaneous units formed included heavy mobile automatic W/T units, light automatic W/T units, mobile air reporting units etc., (MARU). The units were formed at Chigwell.

The existing policy regarding the supply of equipment and the production of mobile and transportable stations was changed in April 1944, when a new unit, the Radio Vehicle Storage Unit, was established at Bowlee. A restatement of the functions of the units concerned was then made. Briefly, the Signals Depots were responsible for installing and testing radio equipment prior to issue to the Radio Vehicle Storage Unit, for executing all major modifications, and for the prototyping of new installations. The new unit was responsible for the storage of, minor modifications to, and testing and completing to scale of new equipment, the servicing and storage of service equipment and the despatch of stations for home and overseas; Chigwell was responsible for the training of units composite mobile and transportable signals units.

APPENDIX THREE

ROLL OF HONOUR FOR HM LANDING SHIP TANK 420
TOTAL OF 320 TRI-SERVICES PERSONNEL WERE LOST IN THIS INCIDENT

Surname	Forename	Age
Rank	Service and Unit	-----

Number	Surname	Forename	Age
1082563	ADAMS	THOMAS	23
Aircraftman 1st Class		Royal Air Force Volunteer Reserve Base Station Radar Unit	
1082625	ALDERSON	AUBREY SYDNEY	40
Aircraftman 1st Class		Royal Air Force Volunteer Reserve	
2082470	ARMSTRONG	DONALD	0
Leading Aircraftman		Royal Air Force Volunteer Reserve Base Station Radar Unit	
2082472	ASH	GREGORY JAMES	40
Leading Aircraftman		Royal Air Force Volunteer Reserve Base Station Radar Unit	
2464535	BAKER	ALEC ALBERT	31
Motor Mechanic		Royal Navy HMLST420	
2475089	BAKER	RONALD JAMES	23
Engine Room Artificer 4th Class		Royal Navy HMLST420	
1083222	BAKER	JOHN	42
Leading Aircraftman		Royal Air Force Volunteer Reserve Base Station Radar Unit	
1083227	BAKER	RAYMOND WILLIAM	24
Leading Aircraftman		Royal Air Force Volunteer Reserve Base Station Radar Unit	
2475119	BALLANTYNE	CHARLES	22
Able Seaman		Royal Navy HMLST420	
1083476	BARTLETT	JAMES CHARLES DOMMETT	30
Sergeant		Royal Air Force Volunteer Reserve Base Station Radar Unit	
1083538	BATES	RAYMOND ARTHUR	22
Leading Aircraftman		Royal Air Force Volunteer Reserve Base Station Radar Unit	
2082474	BATTYE	GEORGE	29
Corporal		Royal Air Force Volunteer Reserve Base Station Radar Unit	
2658757	BAYLISS	RAYMOND LESLIE HOWARD	33
Private		Royal Army Medical Corps 111 General Hospital	
2081867	BERLINER	JACK JOSEPH	0
Leading Aircraftman		Royal Air Force Volunteer Reserve Base Station Radar Unit	
2081868	BINKS	GEORGE JAMES	31
Flight Lieutenant		Royal Air Force Volunteer Reserve Base Station Radar Unit.	
2658784	BLACKMORE	GEORGE WILLIAM	25
Sapper		Royal Engineers-(RAMC) attd.111 General Hospital	
1530138	BOTTOMLEY	COLIN	32
Leading Aircraftman		Royal Air Force Volunteer Reserve Base Station Radar Unit	
2658808	BRACE	JOHN	26
Sapper		Royal Engineers - (RAMC)	
1530299	BRADLEY	SAMUEL GREER	22
Sergeant		Royal Air Force Volunteer Reserve Base Station Radar Unit	
2081873	BROWN	GEORGE BENJAMIN	0
Aircraftman 1st Class		Royal Air Force Volunteer Reserve Base Station Radar Unit	
2081875	BROWN	MATTHEW	0
Leading Aircraftman		Royal Air Force Volunteer Reserve Base Station Radar Unit	
2082476	BRUMPTON	THOMAS KENNETH	0
Leading Aircraftman		Royal Air Force Volunteer Reserve Base Station Radar Unit	

Surname	Forename	Age
Rank	Service and Unit	-----
1530726 BRYANT	PATRICK	24
Sergeant	Royal Air Force Volunteer Reserve Base Station Radar Unit	
2476461 BUSHBY	HARRY HUBERT	43
Petty Officer	Royal Navy HMLST420	
1530988 BUTLER	WILLIAM CHARLES	39
Aircraftman 1st Class	Royal Air Force Volunteer Reserve	
2081880 CAISLEY	LESLIE WILLIAM GEORGE	36
Private	Royal Army Medical Corps	
2774910 CAMP	ALFRED	0
Leading Aircraftman	Royal Air Force Volunteer Reserve Base Station Radar Unit	
2082478 CANNELL	SYDNEY WALTER BRIGGS	0
Sergeant	Royal Air Force Volunteer Reserve Base Station Radar Unit	
2634918 CANNING	WILLIAM JOHN WOODFIELD	38
Leading Aircraftman	Royal Air Force Volunteer Reserve Base Station Radar Unit	
1084081 CARSON	THOMAS WALTER	30
Corporal	Royal Air Force Volunteer Reserve Base Station Radar Unit	
2465764 CARTER	GEOFFREY ALBERT	0
Able Seaman	Royal Navy HMLST420	
2081882 CARTER	ERIC	25
Leading Aircraftman	Royal Air Force Volunteer Reserve Base Station Radar Unit	
1084164 CATHCART	RAYMOND BERTIE	37
Corporal	Royal Air Force Volunteer Reserve Base Station Radar Unit	
1084186 CAWLEY	FRANCIS	31
Corporal	Royal Air Force Volunteer Reserve Base Station Radar Unit	
2082479 CHAMBERS	WILLIAM	22
Leading Aircraftman	Royal Air Force Volunteer Reserve Base Station Radar Unit	
1084321 CHARNLEY	WILLIAM	0
Leading Aircraftman	Royal Air Force Volunteer Reserve Base Station Radar Unit	
2476912 CHORLEY	FREDERICK THOMAS JOHN	42
Leading Stoker	Royal Navy HMLST420	
1084399 CHOWN	WILLIAM ROBERT	47
Leading Aircraftman	Royal Air Force Volunteer Reserve Base Station Radar Unit	
2145568 CLARK	CHARLES	41
Lieutenant	Royal Army Medical Corps	
2081889 CLEARY	ERIC FRANCIS	38
Flying Officer (Unit Accountant)	Royal Air Force Volunteer Reserve Base Station Radar Unit.	
1084689 COLBEAR	GEORGE HAROLD	37
Leading Aircraftman	Royal Air Force Volunteer Reserve Base Station Radar Unit	
2081895 CONLON	JOHN BERNARD	22
Leading Aircraftman	Royal Air Force Volunteer Reserve Base Station Radar Unit	
2081896 COOMBES	REGINALD RICHARD	24
Corporal	Royal Air Force Volunteer Reserve Base Station Radar Unit	
1084917 COOPER	ALLAN EDWARD	27
Sergeant	Royal Canadian Air Force	
1085140 COX	RONALD FREDERICK	34
Leading Aircraftman	Royal Air Force Volunteer Reserve Base Station Radar Unit	
2082482 CRAVEN	HAMMOND	23
Leading Aircraftman	Royal Air Force Volunteer Reserve Base Station Radar Unit	
1085213 CRAWLEY	GEORGE WALTER	0
Flight Sergeant	Royal Air Force Volunteer Reserve Base Station Radar Unit	

Surname	Forename	Age
Rank	Service and Unit	-----
1085218 **CREAN**	JOHN	32
Corporal	Royal Air Force (Auxiliary) Base Station Radar Unit	
231517 **CROFTS**	ARTHUR	39
Aircraftman 1st Class	Royal Air Force Volunteer Reserve Base Station Radar Unit.	
231530 **CROMPTON**	JOSEPH	25
Sergeant	Royal Air Force Volunteer Reserve Base Station Radar Unit.	
2081905 **CURRAN**	JAMES	0
Sergeant	Royal Air Force Volunteer Reserve Base Station Radar Unit	
231867 **DAVIES**	BRINLEY	32
Leading Aircraftman	Royal Air Force Volunteer Reserve Base Station Radar Unit.	
231882 **DAVIES**	EVAN LLOYD	34
Leading Aircraftman	Royal Air Force Volunteer Reserve Base Station Radar Unit	
2082484 **DAVIES**	THOMAS IRWIN	0
Leading Aircraftman	Royal Air Force Volunteer Reserve Base Station Radar Unit	
2145783 **DAVIES**	THOMAS STEPHEN	30
Driver	Royal Army Service Corps(Royal Army Medical Corps)	
2081910 **DAVIES**	JOHN CHARLES	21
Leading Aircraftman	Royal Air Force Volunteer Reserve Base Station Radar Unit	
231982 **DAVISON**	LEONARD FREDERICK	0
Leading Aircraftman	Royal Air Force Volunteer Reserve Base Station Radar Unit	
232052 **DEAN**	KENNETH VICKERY	0
Sergeant	Royal Air Force Base Station Radar Unit.	
232239 **DINES**	JAMES FREDERICK	26
Sergeant	Royal Air Force Volunteer Reserve Base Station Radar Unit	
2478278 **DINSMORE**	ROBERT JOHN	22
Leading Telegraphist	Royal Navy HMLST420.	
232301 **DODDS**	WILLIAM GEORGE	35
Leading Aircraftman	Royal Air Force Volunteer Reserve Base Station Radar Unit	
2081914 **DOWLING**	WILLIAM VICTOR	20
Sub-Lieutenant	Royal Naval Volunteer Reserve HMLST420	
2478406 **DOWMAN**	FRANCIS HENRY	23
Able Seaman	Royal Navy HMLST420	
2478454 **DREDGE**	CHARLES JAMES	27
Stoker 1st Class	Royal Navy HMLST420	
2081917 **DUFF**	ROBERT ALFRED	21
Leading Aircraftman	Royal Air Force Volunteer Reserve Base Station Radar Unit	
2081920 **DUNSTER**	JOHN HENRY	24
Corporal	Royal Air Force Volunteer Reserve Base Station Radar Unit	
2082971 **DURRANT**	HAROLD DAVISON	28
Flying Officer	Royal Canadian Air Force	
2699492 **DUXBURY**	CHATBURN	21
Ordinary Signalman	Royal Navy HMLST420.	
2082487 **EBBS**	HENRY DENNIS ELGAR	0
Flying Officer	Royal Air Force Volunteer Reserve Base Station Radar Unit	
2478702 **EDWARDS**	FREDERICK CHARLES	21
Able Seaman	Royal Navy HM LST420.	
2082488 **EDWARDS**	WILLIAM HENRY	32
Leading Aircraftman	Royal Air Force Volunteer Reserve Base Station Radar Unit	
2081921 **EDWARDS**	DAVID KENNETH VINCENT	31
Leading Aircraftman	Royal Air Force Volunteer Reserve Base Station Radar Unit	

Surname	Forename	Age
Rank	**Service and Unit**	-----
1269503 **ELDER**	**ALASTAIR JOHN BLACK**	23
Leading Aircraftman	Royal Air Force Volunteer Reserve Base Station Radar Unit	
2080754 **ELLIOTT**	**CHARLES EDWARD**	0
Driver	Royal Army Service Corps	
1269626 **ENGLAND**	**JOHN**	44
Flight Sergeant	Royal Air Force Base Station Radar Unit	
1269629 **ENGLISH**	**ERIC DONALD**	23
Leading Aircraftman	Royal Air Force Volunteer Reserve Base Station Radar Unit	
1269693 **EVANS**	**EDMUND JOHN**	24
Corporal	Royal Air Force Volunteer Reserve Base Station Radar Unit.	
1269706 **EVANS**	**ILLTYD ELLIS**	22
Leading Aircraftman	Royal Air Force Volunteer Reserve Base Station Radar Unit	
2658999 **EVERARD**	**GEORGE WILLIAM**	39
Private	Royal Army Medical Corps 111 General Hospital	
2478941 **EVERETT**	**DOUGLAS HAROLD** Mentioned in Despatches	30
Lieut-Commander	Royal Naval Reserve HMLST420	
1269805 **FALLOWS**	**WILLIAM ALFRED**	37
Corporal	Royal Air Force Volunteer Reserve	
1270187 **FOLKARD**	**GEORGE HENRY**	22
Corporal	Royal Air Force Volunteer Reserve	
2108985 **FORD**	**LEONARD CHARLES**	33
Leading Aircraftman	Royal Air Force Volunteer Reserve	
2479277 **FOREMAN**	**SAMUEL**	31
Able Seaman	Royal Navy HM LST.420.	
2081934 **FRANCIS**	**EDWARD HERBERT** [ST JOHN AMBULANCE]	38
Flying Officer	Royal Air Force Volunteer Reserve Base Station Radar Unit	
1270391 **FRASER**	**CHARLES EDWARD**	44
Leading Aircraftman	Royal Air Force Volunteer Reserve Base Station Radar Unit	
1270507 **FULLER**	**KENNETH TERENCE**	27
Leading Aircraftman	Royal Air Force Volunteer Reserve Base Station Radar Unit	
1270580 **GAMBLE**	**FREDERICK GEORGE**	32
Corporal	Royal Air Force Volunteer Reserve Base Station Radar Unit	
2081939 **GATES**	**JOHN THOMAS**	21
Leading Aircraftman	Royal Air Force Volunteer Reserve Base Station Radar Unit	
1270763 **GIBBS**	**WILLIAM HENRY**	22
Aircraftman 1st Class	Royal Air Force Volunteer Reserve Base Station Radar Unit	
2081941 **GIBSON**	**JOHN**	22
Engine Room Artificer 4th Class	Royal Navy HMLST420.	
1270807 **GILDER**	**ALBERT KENNETH**	28
Aircraftman 1st Class	Royal Air Force Volunteer Reserve Base Station Radar Unit	
1270846 **GILL**	**WILLIAM PERCY**	0
Aircraftman 2nd Class	Royal Air Force Volunteer Reserve Base Station Radar Unit	
1270850 **GILLARD**	**DONALD WILLIAM**	45
Corporal	Royal Air Force Base Station Radar Unit B.S.R.U.	
1270894 **GISSANE**	**DENIS JOHN**	0
Sergeant	Royal Air Force Volunteer Reserve Base Station Radar Unit	
2082491 **GOLD**	**ALEXANDER BUCHANAN**	32
Leading Aircraftman	Royal Air Force Volunteer Reserve Base Station Radar Unit	
1798514 **GOMER**	**WILLIAM HENRY**	38
Corporal	Royal Air Force Volunteer Reserve Base Station Radar Unit	
2479919 **GOODWIN**	**WILLIAM**	0
Able Seaman	Royal Navy HMLST420	

Surname	Forename	Age
Rank	Service and Unit	-----
1798665 GRAHAMES	JAMES	41
Aircraftman 1st Class	Royal Air Force Volunteer Reserve Base Station Radar Unit	
2479999 GRANGE	REGINALD	21
Able Seaman	Royal Navy HMLST420	
2082492 GRAY	THOMAS	19
Aircraftman 1st Class	Royal Air Force Volunteer Reserve Base Station Radar Unit.	
2480064 GREEN	FREDERICK DONALD	0
Able Seaman	Royal Navy HMLST420	
1798792 GREEN	WILLIAM HENRY	0
Flight Sergeant	Royal Air Force Volunteer Reserve Base Station Radar Unit.	
2081952 GREENOP	SELBY	32
Flight Lieutenant	Royal Air Force Volunteer Reserve Base Station Radar Unit	
2467938 GREENWOOD	TREVOR	23
Petty Officer Motor Mechanic	Royal Navy HMLST420	
2081954 GREGORY	LEONARD ERIC <u>Mentioned in Despatches</u>	36
Flying Officer	Royal Air Force Base Station Radar Unit.	
1798897 GRIFFITHS	DOUGLAS EDWIN	23
Aircraftman 1st Class	Royal Air Force Volunteer Reserve Base Station Radar Unit.	
1798929 GRIMSHAW	HERBERT PARKINSON	32
Corporal	Royal Air Force Volunteer Reserve Base Station Radar Unit	
2146408 HALIFAX	FREDERICK HENRY THOMAS	20
Driver	Royal Army Service Corps (Royal Army Medical Corps)	
2468177 HARDWICK	SYDNEY JOHN	41
Leading Stoker	Royal Navy HMLST420	
1799421 HARMAN	GEORGE STANLEY	0
Warrant Officer	Royal Air Force Base Station Radar Unit	
2082497 HARVEY	WILLIAM JAMES	28
Corporal	Royal Air Force Volunteer Reserve Base Station Radar Unit	
1799884 HELLON	WILLIAM BURTON	21
Flying Officer	Royal Air Force Volunteer Reserve Base Station Radar Unit.	
2082498 HERBERT	JOHN DOUGLAS	39
Private	Royal Army Medical Corps 111 General Hospital	
2082499 HILDITCH	RUSSELL	30
Aircraftman 1st Class	Royal Air Force Volunteer Reserve Base Station Radar Unit	
2146574 HIORNS	HAROLD	33
Driver	Royal Army Service Corps (Royal Army Medical Corps)	
1800242 HOCKEY	FREDERICK THOMAS	31
Corporal	Royal Air Force Volunteer Reserve Base Station Radar Unit	
1800269 HODGKINSON	GEORGE	32
Sergeant	Royal Air Force Volunteer Reserve Base Station Radar Unit	
1800410 HOLT	JOSEPH ALFRED	21
Leading Aircraftman	Royal Air Force Volunteer Reserve Base Station Radar Unit	
2481442 HOUGHTON	ARTHUR HENRY <u>Distinguished Service Medal</u>	26
Leading Seaman	Royal Navy HMLST420	
1800707 HUGHES	VICTOR KITCHENER	29
Corporal	Royal Air Force Volunteer Reserve Base Station Radar Unit	
2081972 HUGHES	CHARLES FREDERICK	43
Leading Aircraftman	Royal Air Force Volunteer Reserve Base Station Radar Unit	
2081973 HUGHES	DANIEL IFOR	0
Aircraftman 2nd Class	Royal Air Force Volunteer Reserve Base Station Radar Unit	
2081974 HULME	EDMUND JOSEPH	27
Leading Aircraftman	Royal Air Force Volunteer Reserve Base Station Radar Unit	

Surname	Forename	Age
Rank	Service and Unit	-----
1800825 HURST	**GEORGE WILSON**	0
Sergeant	Royal Air Force Volunteer Reserve Base Station Radar Unit	
2081978 HUTTON	**GORDON JOSEPH DAVIE**	31
Corporal	Royal Air Force Volunteer Reserve Base Station Radar Unit	
2481780 INSLEY	**CECIL PHILIP**	19
Leading Stores Assistant	Royal Navy HMLST420	
1800923 IRISH	**EDWIN JAMES**	38
Squadron Leader	Royal Air Force Base Station Radar Unit	
1800924 IRONS	**EDWARD VAUGHAN**	21
Aircraftman 1st Class	Royal Air Force Volunteer Reserve Base Station Radar Unit.	
1801059 JAMES	**The Rev. DEWI HENRI**	28
Chaplain	Royal Air Force Volunteer Reserve	
2481947 JARRETT	**JOHN EDWIN**	26
Petty Officer	Royal Navy HMLST420	
2482074 JOHNSON	**FREDERICK RICHARD ENOCH**	27
Petty Officer Cook (S)	Royal Navy HMLST420	
2082500 JOHNSON	**FREDERICK**	24
Corporal	Royal Air Force Volunteer Reserve Base Station Radar Unit	
2082501 JONES	**IVOR MANSE**	21
Leading Aircraftman	Royal Air Force Volunteer Reserve Base Station Radar Unit.	
1802248 JONES	**ALFRED GEORGE ERNEST**	0
Leading Aircraftman	Royal Air Force Volunteer Reserve	
2146786 JONES	**JOHN GEORGE**	0
Serjeant	Corps of Military Police	
2082502 JUDSON	**CHARLES HENRY**	32
Leading Aircraftman	Royal Air Force Volunteer Reserve Base Station Radar Unit.	
1802454 KAMINSKY	**MORRIS**	25
Corporal	Royal Air Force Volunteer Reserve Base Station Radar Unit	
2453452 KANE	**JOSEPH**	23
Corporal	Royal Air Force Volunteer Reserve Base Station Radar Unit.	
1802579 KENDALL	**ARTHUR JOHN**	24
Leading Aircraftman	Royal Air Force Volunteer Reserve	
2033948 KERR	**ROBERT JOHN**	20
Aircraftman 1st Class	Royal Air Force Volunteer Reserve Base Station Radar Unit	
2081992 KINGE	**JOHN PERCY**	24
Leading Aircraftman	Royal Air Force Volunteer Reserve Base Station Radar Unit	
1802905 KOHN	**CHARLES WILLIAM**	31
Corporal	Royal Air Force Volunteer Reserve Base Station Radar Unit	
1802952 LADBURY	**RONALD OSCAR**	40
Leading Aircraftman	Royal Air Force Volunteer Reserve Base Station Radar Unit	
1803104 LATHAM	**KENNETH SAMUEL**	20
Leading Aircraftman	Royal Air Force Volunteer Reserve Base Station Radar Unit	
1803159 LAWRIE	**JOHN YORKE**	23
Leading Aircraftman	Royal Air Force Volunteer Reserve Base Station Radar Unit	
1803182 LAWSON	**WILLIAM**	38
Leading Aircraftman	Royal Air Force Volunteer Reserve Base Station Radar Unit	
2082001 LEAVEY	**ARTHUR JAMES**	25
Leading Steward	Royal Navy HMLST420	
1803255 LEECH	**JOHN**	21
Aircraftman 2nd Class	Royal Air Force Volunteer Reserve Base Station Radar Unit	
2469740 LEMON	**KENNETH ROBERTS**	0
Leading Motor Mechanic	Royal Navy HMLST420	

Surname	Forename	Age
Rank	Service and Unit	-----
1803411 LEWIS	RONALD GEOFFREY	25
Leading Aircraftman	Royal Air Force Volunteer Reserve Base Station Radar Unit	
2082004 LIGHT	LESLIE REX	0
Private	Army Catering Corps	
2082006 LIGHTFOOT	HORACE	38
Leading Aircraftman	Royal Air Force Volunteer Reserve Base Station Radar Unit	
2483235 LINSEY	PERCY RAYMOND	19
Assistant Steward	Royal Navy HMLST420	
2483289 LLOYD	WILLIAM EDWARD	22
Leading Stoker	Royal Navy HMLST420	
2147027 LONG	LESLIE	34
Driver	Royal Army Service Corps (Royal Army Medical Corps	
1079080 LYTH	ERIC	24
Aircraftman 2nd Class	Royal Air Force Base Station Radar Unit.	
1079242 MACDONALD	ALEXANDER FRASER	22
Leading Aircraftman	Royal Air Force Volunteer Reserve Base Station Radar Unit	
1079317 MACE	LAURENCE HENRY	35
Leading Aircraftman	Royal Air Force Volunteer Reserve Base Station Radar Unit.	
1079386 MACGREGOR	ANGUS JOHN	24
Leading Aircraftman	Royal Air Force Volunteer Reserve Base Station Radar Unit	
2083307 MacLAREN	ALEXANDER	32
Aircraftman 1st Class	Royal Air Force Volunteer Reserve Base Station Radar Unit	
2082506 MADDISON	WILLIAM	43
Leading Aircraftman	Royal Air Force Volunteer Reserve Base Station Radar Unit	
1079848 MALLINSON	HARRY	30
Warrant Officer	Royal Air Force Volunteer Reserve Base Station Radar Unit	
1079931 MARK TERENCE	NORMAN	27
Corporal	Royal Air Force Volunteer Reserve Base Station Radar Unit	
2082020 MARSHALL	WILLIAM JAMES	0
Sergeant	Royal Canadian Air Force	
2356641 MARSHALL	PERCY	43
Leading Aircraftman	Royal Air Force Volunteer Reserve Base Station Radar Unit	
1079993 MARSHALL	GORDON	20
Leading Aircraftman	Royal Air Force Volunteer Reserve Base Station Radar Unit.	
1080057 MARTIN	LEONARD SYDNEY	24
Sergeant	Royal Air Force Volunteer Reserve Base Station Radar Unit	
2657122 MASTERS	FREDERICK	27
Engine Room Artificer 4th Class	Royal Navy HMLST420	
2484174 MASTERS	SIDNEY HERBERT	0
Telegraphist	Royal Navy HMLST420	
1076648 MAYS	GEORGE CLAYDON	32
Sergeant	Royal Air Force Volunteer Reserve Base Station Radar Unit	
1079157 McCARTHY	DOMINIC	25
Sergeant	Royal Air Force Volunteer Reserve Base Station Radar Unit	
1079274 McDONALD	JOHN GALT	0
Corporal	Royal Air Force Volunteer Reserve Base Station Radar Unit	
2082010 McDONALD	HARRY	27
Sergeant	Royal Air Force Base Station Radar Unit.	
1079368 McGONAGLE	CHARLES ERNEST	35
Aircraftman 1st Class	Royal Air Force Volunteer Reserve Base Station Radar Unit	

Surname	Forename	Age
Rank	Service and Unit	-----
1079371 **McGOW**	**JOHN ALEXANDER**	30
Leading Aircraftman	Royal Air Force Volunteer Reserve Base Station Radar Unit	
2082505 **McGRATH**	**JACK**	29
Leading Aircraftman	Royal Air Force Volunteer Reserve Base Station Radar Unit	
1079468 **McKEAN**	**GORDON**	23
Aircraftman 1st Class	Royal Air Force Volunteer Reserve Base Station Radar Unit	
1079475 **McKEEMAN**	**The Rev. ERIC WALTER**	40
Chaplain	Royal Air Force Volunteer Reserve	
2483807 **McLEOD**	**WILLIAM RATTRAY**	24
Steward Royal Navy	HMLST420	
2483821 **McMIKEN**	**GEORGE ERIC**	22
Leading Seaman	Royal Navy HMLST420	
2082507 **MIDDLEMISS**	**JAMES ALBERT**	22
Leading Aircraftman	Royal Air Force Volunteer Reserve Base Station Radar Unit	
2082508 **MOFFETT**	**HAROLD**	21
Leading Aircraftman	Royal Air Force Volunteer Reserve Base Station Radar Unit	
1077055 **MOONEY**	**JAMES**	28
Sergeant	Royal Air Force Volunteer Reserve Base Station Radar Unit	
1077058 **MOORE**	**ALBERT JOSEPH**	30
Leading Aircraftman	Royal Air Force Volunteer Reserve Base Station Radar Unit	
2082509 **MOORE**	**JOHN ALEXANDER**	22
Sergeant	Royal Air Force Volunteer Reserve Base Station Radar Unit	
1077186 **MORRELL**	**FREDERICK REGINALD**	0
Leading Aircraftman	Royal Air Force Volunteer Reserve Base Station Radar Unit	
2484777 **MORRIS**	**HENRY**	23
Leading Stoker	Royal Navy HMLST420.	
1077217 **MORRIS**	**JOSEPH**	0
Leading Aircraftman	Royal Air Force Volunteer Reserve Base Station Radar Unit	
1077247 **MORRISS**	**THOMAS GEOFFREY**	0
Flying Officer	Royal Air Force Volunteer Reserve Base Station Radar Unit	
1077350 **MUDD**	**JOHN THOMAS**	25
Corporal	Royal Air Force	
1077473 **MURRELL**	**COLIN**	24
Leading Aircraftman	Royal Air Force Volunteer Reserve Base Station Radar Unit	
2082510 **NICHOLLS**	**REGINALD DAVID**	24
Leading Aircraftman	Royal Air Force Volunteer Reserve Base Station Radar Unit	
2034123 **NORRIS**	**FREDERICK**	33
Leading Aircraftman	Royal Air Force Volunteer Reserve Base Station Radar Unit	
1803619 **O'NEILL**	**DAVID HENRY**	26
Sergeant	Royal Air Force Volunteer Reserve Base Station Radar Unit.	
1803697 **OWEN**	**ARTHUR** British Empire Medal	34
Corporal	Royal Air Force	
1803869 **PARKES**	**GEORGE RAYMOND**	0
Aircraftman 2nd Class	Royal Air Force Volunteer Reserve Base Station Radar Unit	
1803910 **PARRY**	**ARTHUR CHARLES**	0
Corporal	Royal Air Force Volunteer Reserve Base Station Radar Unit	
1803930 **PARSONS**	**IVOR HENRY**	28
Leading Aircraftman	Royal Air Force Volunteer Reserve Base Station Radar Unit	
2082048 **PARTRIDGE**	**ROBERT HENRY**	24
Leading Aircraftman	Royal Air Force Volunteer Reserve Base Station Radar Unit	
2082050 **PAYNE**	**GEORGE HORACE**	28
Corporal	Royal Air Force Volunteer Reserve Base Station Radar Unit.	

Surname	Forename	Age
Rank	Service and Unit	
2485796 **PEARSON**	**EDWARD**	0
Stoker 1st Class	Royal Navy HMLST420	
2034182 **PETRIE**	**ALBERT**	34
Corporal	Royal Air Force Volunteer Reserve Base Station Radar Unit.	
1804281 **PHILIPSON**	**DENIS JAMES**	23
Corporal	Royal Air Force Volunteer Reserve Base Station Radar Unit.	
2082512 **PHILLIBEN**	**MICHAEL**	31
Corporal	Royal Air Force Volunteer Reserve Base Station Radar Unit	
2082513 **PHIPPS**	**PATRICK JOHN EDNIC**	24
Leading Aircraftman	Royal Air Force Volunteer Reserve Base Station Radar Unit	
2082053 **PILKINGTON**	**WALTER**	25
Sergeant	Royal Air Force Volunteer Reserve Base Station Radar Unit	
2082514 **PIPE**	**BENJAMIN**	40
Corporal	Royal Air Force Volunteer Reserve Base Station Radar Unit	
2082515 **PLATER**	**JOHN EDWARD**	36
Driver	Royal Army Service Corps	
1804475 **POLLEY**	**ALLAN JOHN**	21
Leading Aircraftman	Royal Air Force Volunteer Reserve Base Station Radar Unit	
2082056 **POOLE**	**GORDON FREDERICK**	33
Leading Aircraftman	Royal Air Force Volunteer Reserve Base Station Radar Unit	
2486192 **PORTER**	**KENNETH WILLIAM**	19
Assistant Cook (S)	Royal Navy HMLST420	
2698181 **POSTLETHWAITE**	**DAVID**	36
Corporal	Royal Air Force Volunteer Reserve	
2486234 **POWELL**	**PHILIP WILLIAM**	18
Stoker 1st Class	Royal Navy HMLST420	
2486268 **PRESS**	**LESLIE BERNARD**	31
Stoker 1st Class	Royal Navy HMLST420	
2082058 **PRICE**	**JAMES HENRY**	21
Leading Aircraftman	Royal Air Force Volunteer Reserve Base Station Radar Unit	
2082516 **PRINGLE**	**ARNOLD WILLIAM**	38
Stores Assistant	Royal Navy HMLST420	
2939928 **RAYMER**	**DONALD**	21
Leading Aircraftman	Royal Air Force Volunteer Reserve Base Station Radar Unit	
2939955 **READ**	**VERNON REX**	24
Sergeant	Royal Air Force Volunteer Reserve Base Station Radar Unit	
2939963 **READY**	**NORMAN FRANKLAND**	0
Leading Aircraftman	Royal Canadian Air Force	
2082060 **REDDING**	**WILLIAM HENRY**	40
Warrant Officer	Royal Air Force Base Station Radar Unit	
2940019 **REES**	**STANLEY PERCY**	22
Leading Aircraftman	Royal Air Force Volunteer Reserve Base Station Radar Unit	
2486643 **RENDLE**	**ERNEST EDWARD LETHBRIDGE**	30
Stoker 1st Class	Royal Navy HMLST420	
2082517 **RIDER**	**VICTOR JAMES**	26
Driver	Royal Army Service Corps	
2940273 **RIGBY**	**LESLIE ELLIOTT**	25
Leading Aircraftman	Royal Air Force Volunteer Reserve Base Station Radar Unit	
2564070 **RILEY**	**JOHN TURTON**	20
Signalman	Royal New Zealand Navy HMLST420	
2082518 **ROBINSON**	**FRANCIS WILLIAM**	31
Leading Aircraftman	Royal Air Force Volunteer Reserve Base Station Radar Unit	

Surname	Forename	Age
Rank	Service and Unit	-----
2486968 ROBLEY	**THOMAS PETER**	30
Able Seaman	Royal Naval Volunteer Reserve HMLST420	
2940483 RODGER	**JOHN ADAMSON**	20
Aircraftman 2nd Class	Royal Air Force Volunteer Reserve	
2082069 ROPER	**EDWARD CHARLES**	38
Leading Aircraftman	Royal Air Force Volunteer Reserve Base Station Radar Unit	
2487053 ROSBOROUGH	**JOHN ALEXANDER**	20
Able Seaman	Royal Navy HMLST420	
2082519 ROWLEY	**ROBERT BIRKLEY GRENVILLE**	23
Leading Aircraftman	Royal Air Force Volunteer Reserve Base Station Radar Unit	
2082073 RUDDERHAM	**ARTHUR JAMES**	0
Leading Aircraftman	Royal Air Force Volunteer Reserve Base Station Radar Unit	
2940761 RUTH	**THOMAS ELIAS**	39
Leading Aircraftman	Royal Air Force Volunteer Reserve Base Station Radar Unit	
2940763 RUTHERFORD	**ARTHUR**	24
Corporal	Royal Air Force Volunteer Reserve Base Station Radar Unit	
2082074 RUTHERFORD	**JOHN**	33
Private	Corps of Military Police	
2735070 SALMON	**ANTHONY**	21
Flying Officer	Royal Air Force Volunteer Reserve	
2940842 SALTER	**FRANK**	0
Leading Aircraftman	Royal Air Force Volunteer Reserve	
2940959 SCANLON	**LAURENCE**	21
Leading Aircraftman	Royal Air Force Volunteer Reserve	
2487505 SEAMAN	**PHILIP WALTER**	20
Stoker 1st Class	Royal Navy HMLST420	
2082520 SEAMAN	**PERCY HERBERT**	34
Leading Aircraftman	Royal Air Force Volunteer Reserve Base Station Radar Unit	
2082078 SEATON	**WALTER**	24
Private	Corps of Military Police	
2941095 SEDGWICK	**MAURICE**	33
Sergeant	Royal Air Force Volunteer Reserve Base Station Radar Unit	
2941122 SELWAY	**FRANK**	21
Leading Aircraftman	Royal Air Force Volunteer Reserve	
2148035 SHAW	**BENJAMIN**	34
Lance Corporal	Corps of Military Police H.Q. 335 Provost Coy.	
1806997 SHEAD	**PERCIVAL JAMES**	23
Leading Aircraftman	Royal Air Force Volunteer Reserve	
2487621 SHEARER	**GEORGE PETER**	23
Shipwright 4th Class	Royal Navy HMLST420	
2082081 SHICKLE	**JAMES HENRY**	0
Leading Aircraftman	Royal Air Force Volunteer Reserve Base Station Radar Unit	
2659564 SHILTON	**JOHN**	41
Private	Corps of Military Police	
2082082 SHINGLER	**ROY**	22
Aircraftman 1st Class	Royal Air Force Volunteer Reserve Base Station Radar Unit	
2082083 SINTON	**HENRY**	0
Leading Aircraftman	Royal Air Force Volunteer Reserve Base Station Radar Unit.	
2082521 SKARDON	**JAMES JOHN**	44
Driver	Royal Army Service Corps	
1807252 SKILLINGS	**BERNARD**	35
Leading Aircraftman	Royal Air Force Volunteer Reserve	

Surname	Forename	Age
Rank	Service and Unit	-----
1807264 SKINNER	WALTER HENRY	22
Leading Aircraftman	Royal Air Force Volunteer Reserve	
1807274 SLACK	IVOR	22
Leading Aircraftman	Royal Air Force Volunteer Reserve	
1807291 SLATER	WALTER JAMES	34
Leading Aircraftman	Royal Air Force Volunteer Reserve	
2659584 SMITH	ALBERT GEORGE	45
Private	Corps of Military Police	
2082522 SMITH	ALAN JOHN	37
Leading Aircraftman	Royal Air Force Volunteer Reserve Base Station Radar Unit	
1807568 SMITH	ROBERT TURNER	44
Aircraftman 2nd Class	Royal Air Force Volunteer Reserve Base Station Radar Unit	
2488111 SOUTHWARD	THOMAS	31
Leading Stoker	Royal Navy HMLST420	
2082523 SPARKES	GEORGE EDWARD	36
Leading Aircraftman	Royal Air Force Volunteer Reserve Base Station Radar Unit	
1807724 SPEARS	ALBERT EDWARD	22
Leading Aircraftman	Royal Air Force Volunteer Reserve Base Station Radar Unit	
1807734 SPENCE	EDWARD PEMBERTON	0
Leading Aircraftman	Royal Air Force Volunteer Reserve	
1807766 SPILLMAN	CHARLES JOHN	25
Corporal	Royal Air Force Volunteer Reserve	
2148200 STAITE	WILLIAM EDGAR	39
Private	Corps of Military Police	
2082092 STANSFIELD	ERIC LEES	29
Aircraftman 1st Class	Royal Air Force Volunteer Reserve Base Station Radar Unit	
2082093 STEAD	EDWARD	42
Leading Aircraftman	Royal Air Force Volunteer Reserve Base Station Radar Unit	
2472833 STEPHENS	ALBERT	0
Stoker 1st Class	Royal Navy HMLST420	
2659623 STEWARD	WILLIAM HORACE	45
Private	Corps of Military Police	
1808045 STIRZAKER	JAMES ROWLAND	33
Corporal	Royal Air Force Volunteer Reserve	
1808068 STOCKWELL	CYRIL HENRY	33
Sergeant	Royal Air Force Volunteer Reserve	
2488518 SULLIVAN	LESLIE ROY	20
Ordinary Telegraphist	Royal Navy HMLST420	
2148266 SUNDERLAND	JOHN	29
Private	Corps of Military Police	
2082524 SWEENEY	JOHN	27
Corporal	Royal Air Force Volunteer Reserve Base Station Radar Unit	
2082102 TAMS	ALBERT WILLIAM	0
Leading Aircraftman	Royal Air Force Volunteer Reserve Base Station Radar Unit	
2659640 TANNER	THOMAS	39
Private	Corps of Military Police 335 H.Q. Coy.	
2082103 TATE	EDWARD JAMES	23
Leading Aircraftman	Royal Air Force Volunteer Reserve Base Station Radar Unit.	
2488748 TAYLOR	WILLIAM	26
Able Seaman	Royal Navy HMLST420	
2659644 TAYLOR	FRANK WALLACE	20
Private	Royal Army Medical Corps 111 General Hospital	

Surname		Forename	Age
Rank		Service and Unit	
1808540	TAYLOR	**LEONARD REGINALD OSBORNE**	22
Sergeant		Royal Air Force Volunteer Reserve	
2082104	TAYLOR	**DONALD DAVID MACKENZIE**	26
Corporal		Royal Canadian Air Force	
2659651	TEDDER	**FREDERICK CHARLES**	37
Private		Corps of Military Police	
1808689	THOMAS	**WILLIAM HERBERT**	0
Aircraftman 1st Class		Royal Air Force Volunteer Reserve	
2082525	THOMPSON	**LESLIE NORMAN**	37
Leading Aircraftman		Royal Air Force Volunteer Reserve Base Station Radar Unit	
1808709	THOMPSON	**FRANCIS WILLIAM SNOWDEN**	24
Aircraftman 1st Class		Royal Air Force Volunteer Reserve	
2082526	THORBURN	**ALAN**	39
Leading Aircraftman		Royal Air Force Volunteer Reserve Base Station Radar Unit	
2034405	THURMAN	**ROY**	0
Leading Aircraftman		Royal Air Force Volunteer Reserve Base Station Radar Unit	
1808838	TICKLE	**DONALD WINGFIELD**	20
Aircraftman 1st Class		Royal Air Force Volunteer Reserve	
2489214	TURNBULL	**HARRY**	21
Able Seaman		Royal Navy HMLST420	
1809109	TURNER	**ARTHUR**	0
Corporal		Royal Air Force	
2082115	TYLER	**LESLIE JOHN**	0
Flight Lieutenant		Royal Air Force Volunteer Reserve Base Station Radar Unit	
2489324	UTTLEY	**FRED**	0
Able Seaman		Royal Navy HMLST420	
2082117	VARDEY	**ERIC**	24
Leading Aircraftman		Royal Air Force Volunteer Reserve Base Station Radar Unit	
2082529	VIVIAN	**JACK CYRIL**	0
Leading Aircraftman		Royal Air Force Volunteer Reserve Base Station Radar Unit.	
2148454	WAITE	**FRANK WILLIAM**	20
Driver		Royal Army Service Corps (Royal Army Medical Corps 111 General Hospital)	
1809507	WALKER	**WILLIAM HENRY**	35
Leading Aircraftman		Royal Air Force Volunteer Reserve	
2082119	WALLER	**EDWIN**	36
Leading Aircraftman		Royal Air Force Volunteer Reserve Base Station Radar Unit	
2775009	WALLWORTH	**PHILIP**	23
Leading Aircraftman		Royal Air Force Volunteer Reserve Base Station Radar Unit	
2082531	WARD	**FREDERICK**	42
Leading Aircraftman		Royal Air Force Volunteer Reserve Base Station Radar Unit	
1809639	WARDROBE	**PETER**	30
Leading Aircraftman		Royal Air Force Volunteer Reserve	
2659726	WEBB	**BENJAMIN ROBERT**	37
Private		Corps of Military Police	
2489730	WEBB	**ALBERT EDWIN DERRICK**	23
Cook (S)		Royal Navy HMLST420	
1531195	WEINBERG	**ALEC**	36
Leading Aircraftman		Royal Air Force Volunteer Reserve	
2082125	WENDON	**WILLIAM EBER**	42
Wing Commander		Royal Air Force	

Surname	Forename	Age
Rank	Service and Unit	-----
2082127 WHATT	WILLIAM SKELTON	22
Leading Aircraftman	Royal Air Force Volunteer Reserve Base Station Radar Unit	
2691836 WHEELER	RONALD	33
Corporal	Royal Air Force Volunteer Reserve Base Station Radar Unit	
2082129 WHEELER	WILLIAM EVAN	36
Leading Aircraftman	Royal Air Force Volunteer Reserve Base Station Radar Unit.	
2082532 WHITTAKER	ARTHUR	39
Aircraftman 1st Class	Royal Air Force Volunteer Reserve Base Station Radar Unit	
2659745 WHITTAKER	NORMAN JOHN	39
Private	Royal Army Medical Corps 111 General Hospital	
2082533 WHITTLE	SYDNEY	31
Leading Aircraftman	Royal Air Force Volunteer Reserve Base Station Radar Unit	
2214561 WILCOX	WILLIAM ARTHUR	23
Aircraftman 2nd Class	Royal Air Force Volunteer Reserve Base Station Radar Unit	
1531568 WILKINGS	SYDNEY FRANK	23
Leading Aircraftman	Royal Air Force Volunteer Reserve	
2490111 WILLIAMS	EDWARD CHARLES	0
Stoker 1st Class	Royal Navy HMLST420	
1531726 WILLIAMS	WILLIAM SPENCER	0
Aircraftman 2nd Class	Royal Air Force Volunteer Reserve	
2490307 WILSON	REGINALD ATCHESON	22
Stoker 1st Class	Royal Navy HMLST420	
2474109 WILSON	ARTHUR QUINN	0
Leading Motor Mechanic	Royal Navy HMLST420	
2490394 WOOD	ARTHUR	21
Stoker 1st Class	Royal Navy HMLST420	
2082535 WYLDE	RONALD	25
Corporal	Royal Air Force Base Station Radar Unit	
1532264 YOUNG	EDWIN WILFRED JAMES	26
Sergeant	Royal Air Force Volunteer Reserve	
1532297 YOUNG	WILLIAM GRAHAM	24
Aircraftman 1st Class	Royal Air Force Volunteer Reserve	
1532275 YOUNG	JOHN JEFFREY	23
Leading Aircraftman	Royal Air Force Volunteer Reserve	
2082140 ZELLER	ERIC SPENCER	39
Corporal	Royal Air Force Volunteer Reserve Base Station Radar Unit	

A PRAYER FOR THE FALLEN

Prayer offered for the 75th Anniversary of D-Day - Courtesy of the Church of England.
Lord of the nations,
we honour the bravery and sacrifice of those who served.
Grant us similar courage to recognise and restrain evil in our own day,
and may those who lead the nations of the world
work together to defend human liberty,
that we may live peaceably one with another.
This we ask in the name of the Prince of Peace,
our Saviour Jesus Christ.
Amen.

"Victory in Europe" A postcard issued by 2nd Tactical Air Force Royal Air Force

BIBLIOGRAPHY

The Blitz then and Now Volume 3 ISBN 0900913 58 4 Printers Plaistow Press Editor Winston G Ramsey
Not All Airmen Fly -The Story of RAF Chigwell by Jenny Filby and Geoff Clark Published by Epping Forest District Council 1994 Printed by GB Print and Graphics.
The Official War Dairy (originally marked Secret but now declassified) edited reports on pages 187 and 188 http://ww2talk.com/index.php?threads/lst-420.11941/page-3
Hampshire Telegraph Portsmouth, Hampshire, England 11 April 1947
Ballymena Weekly Telegraph Ballymena, Antrim, Northern Ireland 30 December 1949
Baptism Records Christ Church, Barnet, England.
General Records Office Marriage Record Edward H Francis & Esther Elisabeth Jorgensen.
Birth Record Esther Jorgenson Frederiksberg, Denmark on 17 May 1907.
The 1939 Register
The 1911 Census
General Records Office Civil Registration Death Index
Probate Register 1945
Air Publication 3237 The Second World War 1939-1945 Royal Air Force Signals
Internet Records –
Prayer for D-Day Church of England

18//08/2023	*Aerial Vol 2 No 4 Sept 1945* - Contributed by Roger Smoothy for his father C/MX 107794 Leading Writer Peter Smoothy RN 9th LST Flotilla http://www.navsource.org/archives/10/16/160420.htm
11/08/2023	www.therafatomahabeach.com
08/08/2023	https://wrecksite.eu
08/08/2023	https://www.britannica.com/technology/landing-ship-tank
20/12/2023	http://ww2talk.com/index.php?threads/lst-420.11941/page-3 Post by Michel Sabarly
21/08/2023	www.wrecksite.eu
21/08/2023	www.uboat.net
21/08/2023	Belgians-remember-them.eu
21/08/2023	https://www.findagrave.com/memorial/13947163/edwardherbertfrancis
21/08/2023	https://www.cwgc.org/find-records/find-war-dead/casualty-details/2368703/arthur-harry-browne/
21/08/2023	https://www.cwgc.org/find-records/find-war-dead/casualty-details/3144503/helen-maud-thompson/
21/08/2023	https://www.cwgc.org/visit-us/find-cemeteries-memorials/cemetery-details/4004896/potters-bar-urban-district/
21/08/2023	https://www.cwgc.org/find-records/find-war-dead/casualty-details/2369596/victor-coleman/
21/08/2023	https://www.cwgc.org/visit-us/find-cemeteries-memorials/cemetery-details/144703/portsmouth-naval-memorial/
21/08/2023	https://www.cwgc.org/find-records/find-war-dead/casualty-details/2081934/edward-herbert-francis/#&gid=1&pid=1
21/08/2023	https://www.cwgc.org/find-records/find-war-dead/casualty-details/2081934/edward-herbert-francis/#&gid=1&pid=2
21/08/2023	https://www.cwgc.org/find-records/find-war-dead/casualty-details/2368703/arthur-harry-browne/
21/08/2023	https://www.cwgc.org/visit-us/find-cemeteries-memorials/cemetery-details/144703/portsmouth-naval-memorial/
06/08/2023	https://www.therafatomahabeach.com/standard-types-of-mobile-signals-units/

Other Heritage Books by Brian L Porter

St John Ambulance and The Ilford Harrison Gibson Fire 1959, A Night to Remember
Published July 2023	ISBN 978-1-9196468-2-4

St John Ambulance Edmonton, Remembrance & Recognition
Published December 2023	ISBN 978-1-9196468-1-7

St John Ambulance Ilford, Its Beginnings, Its Founders and Its Members
Published May 2023	ISBN 978-1-9196468-0-0

For more information on availability and cost please contact the author on the following email addresses:

Brian.Porter@sja.org.uk or Porterb@sky.com